LEADERSHIP SECRETS
OF JESUS

by
Mike Murdock

Tulsa, Oklahoma

Leadership Secrets of Jesus
ISBN 1-56292-163-0
Copyright © 1996 by Mike Murdock
P. O. Box 99
Dallas, Texas 75221

Published by Honor Books
P. O. Box 55388
Tulsa, Oklahoma 74155

Table of Contents

Preface

I love to see people *succeed* with their life.

And so does God, the Creator.

As the artist treasures his painting and the master craftsman the quality of the violin he created, so our Maker cherishes the dreams, goals, excellence of life, and the happiness you and I are to enjoy.

Through searching diligently for principles for successful living, I was suddenly made aware of these *two forces:* the person of Jesus and the principles He set in motion. The *combined* power of these two influences I call the **"Way of the Winner."**

Winners are simply ex-losers who got *mad*. They got tired of failure. THE DAY YOU GET ANGRY AT YOUR FAILURES IS THE DAY YOU START WINNING. Winning doesn't start around you — it begins INSIDE you.

HAPPINESS BEGINS BETWEEN YOUR EARS. *Your mind is the drawing room for tomorrow's circumstances.* What happens in your mind will happen in time. *Mind-management* is the first priority for the overcomer. "...whatsoever things are true, whatsoever things are honest, whatsoever things are just, whatsoever things are pure, whatsoever things are lovely, whatsoever things are of good report; if there be any virtue, and if there be any praise, think on these things" (Philippians 4:8).

The *system* I found in the Bible *worked.* It has multiplied my joy by increasing my ability to succeed a thousand times over. The Leadership Secrets of Jesus which follow contain this wisdom for living.

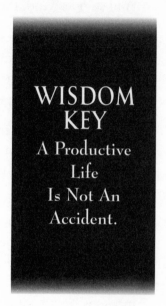

WISDOM
KEY
A Productive
Life
Is Not An
Accident.

Circle today's date on your calendar. Declare that the happiest and most productive days of your life are beginning TODAY! Never, never, never quit. You may BE MINUTES FROM YOUR MIRACLE.

I wrote this book for *you.* I pray that each page will give the *added edge* you need to make your life happier and more fulfilling than ever before.

PART I

LEADERSHIP SECRETS
FOR TOTAL SUCCESS

Jesus Was A Problem-Solver

"Let every one of us please his neighbour for his good to edification."

ROMANS 15:2

Everyone has problems.

Your success and happiness in life depend on your willingness to help someone solve their problem. *Successful people are simply problem-solvers.* A successful attorney solves *legal* problems. Doctors solve *physical* problems. The automobile mechanic solves *car* problems.

Jesus was a problem-solver.

Thousands were burdened with guilt because of their sins. Jesus offered *forgiveness.* Thousands were spiritually starved. He said, "I am the Bread of Life (John 6:35)." Hundreds had bodies riddled with sickness and disease. Jesus "...went about doing good, and healing all that were oppressed of the devil" (Acts 10:38). Many were possessed with evil spirits. Jesus set them *free.*

11

Jesus had something others needed.

He solved their problems. That's why thousands sat for days as He taught them concerning the laws of God and how to have extraordinary relationships with other people.

His products were boldly declared. Eternal life. Joy. Inner peace. Forgiveness. Healing and health. Financial freedom. Take an inventory of yourself. What do you have to offer someone? What do you *enjoy* doing? *What would you attempt to do if you knew it was impossible to fail?*

WISDOM KEY
Everything God Created Is A Solution To A Problem.

You are not an accident. God planned your birth. "Before I formed thee in the belly I knew thee; and before thou camest forth out of the womb I sanctified thee, and I ordained thee" (Jeremiah 1:5).

Everything God makes is a solution to a problem. Every person God created is a solution to a problem. God wanted a love relationship. So, He created Adam. Adam was lonely. So, God created Eve. This is the golden thread that links creation.

Leadership Secret 1

Think of your *contribution* to another as an *assignment* from God. A lawyer is assigned to his client. A wife is *assigned* to her husband. Parents are *assigned* to their children. Employees are *assigned* to their boss.

Your assignment is always to a person or a people.

For example, Moses was assigned to the Israelites. Aaron was assigned to Moses.

Your assignment will always *solve a problem*. Your life is a solution to someone in trouble. Find those who need you and what you have to offer. Build your life around that contribution.

Jesus did.

Prayer

Father, help me to be a problem-solver. Give me Your eyes to find those who need me and help me identify how I can help them. Thank You for creating me to be a solution to a problem. In Jesus' name, amen.

Questions

What specific problem have you recently struggled with but successfully resolved?

How can you help others apply to their own situation what you learned in solving your problem?

How can you make a positive contribution during the coming week in the life of someone to whom you are assigned?

Jesus Believed In His Product

"Be thou diligent to know the state of thy flocks, and look well to thy herds."

PROVERBS 27:23

Doubt is deadly.

Have you ever walked into a room and felt anger in the atmosphere? Have you ever walked into a room and felt love and energy and excitement? Of course! *Your thoughts have presence.* They are like currents moving through the air. Those thoughts are capable of *drawing people toward you or driving people away from you.*

Your attitude is always sensed. You will never succeed in any business unless you really believe in that business. You must believe in the product you are promoting. *Your doubts will eventually surface.*

Look at the life of Jesus. He believed He could *change* people. He believed that His product would *satisfy* people.

15

"Whosoever drinketh of this water shall thirst again: But whosoever drinketh of the water that I shall give him shall never thirst; but the water that I shall give him shall be in him a well of water springing up into everlasting life" (John 4:13,14).

What makes you believe in your product? Product knowledge.

His product was life. "The thief cometh not, but for to steal, and to kill, and to destroy: I am come that they might have life, and that they might have it more abundantly" (John 10:10).

WISDOM KEY

Whatever You Have Been Given Is What Someone Needs.

Jesus saw the damaged products. He knew He was their connection for repair. Nobody could take His place and He knew it. "My sheep hear my voice, and I know them, and they follow me" (John 10:27).

You must take the time and make the effort to *know your product.* It may bore you or even seem unnecessary. You may be anxious to sell your product, pocket the profit, and get on with your life. *But success just does not happen that way.*

A lawyer must study new laws. A doctor must keep well-read on the latest journals concerning the body and new diseases. A policeman has to study his weapons, the laws of his community, his rights, and the mind-set of criminals. If he does not study this, he knows he is "a dead man in the streets." His life is on the line.

Don't expect to succeed unless you are thoroughly informed about your product.

Are you discouraged by your present job? Are you feeling a bit hopeless? Then I suggest you ask yourself some real soul-searching and honest questions. How much *time* have you spent cultivating an awareness of your business? Do you *use* your product? How many hours each day have you *invested in becoming informed?* Are you so busy trying to "make a buck" that you really have not developed a powerful understanding and confidence in what you are doing?

Jesus was very busy. He was teaching, preaching, traveling,

WISDOM KEY

Information Breeds Confidence.

performing miracles, and mentoring the unlearned. However, He always took the time to get alone with His Father and renew His understanding of His purpose, His plan, and His product. "My people are destroyed for lack of knowledge" (Hosea 4:6).

Jesus believed in His product.

Prayer

Father, thank You for placing inside of me diligence to know my product/service/career to its fullest extent. I know that You have given me ideas and methods for helping other people. Teach me to develop a powerful understanding and confidence in what I am promoting. In Jesus' name, amen.

Questions

In three sentences or less how would you define your product?

What resources do you use to keep yourself informed about your product and field of expertise?

How much time do you spend each week in prayer for your organization?

Jesus Never Misrepresented His Product

"Recompense to no man evil for evil. Provide things honest in the sight of all men."

ROMANS 12:17

Liars are eventually exposed.

It may take weeks or even months, but the truth always surfaces. "He that covereth his sins shall not prosper" (Proverbs 28:13).

Anyone who does business with you wants the truth — the total truth. People fear misrepresentation.

Jesus had the greatest product on earth — salvation. He offered the human race an opportunity to have a relationship with God. He spoke of heaven and angels. "In my Father's house are many mansions: if it were not so, I would have told you" (John 14:2).

But, He never painted a distorted picture.

He warned His disciples of *persecution*. "But beware of men: for they will deliver you up to the councils, and they will scourge you in their synagogues" (Matthew 10:17).

He spoke of their *afflictions*. "Then shall they deliver you up to be afflicted, and shall kill you: and ye shall be hated of all nations for my name's sake" (Matthew 24:9).

He spoke of *loneliness*. "The foxes have holes, and the birds of the air have nests; but the Son of man hath not where to lay his head" (Matthew 8:20).

WISDOM KEY
Give Another What He Cannot Find Anywhere Else, And He Will Keep Returning.

Jesus believed in preparing people for any possible situation that could happen. He was honest. His teaching was far more than a "pie in the sky" philosophy.

Listen to the apostle Paul. "Of the Jews five times received I forty stripes save one. Thrice was I beaten with rods, once I was stoned, thrice I suffered shipwreck, a night and a day I have been in the deep" (2 Corinthians 11:24,25).

This certainly does not sound like the most ideal sales talk to a group of students in Bible school! Paul did not misrepresent his product either.

Jesus spoke to many people of the good things and the benefits of what He offered, but He was also quick to talk to them about the *total* picture. Then, they would be prepared to face their trials.

Address the benefits. Focus on the advantages that your product or your business will offer to another person. But never forget *that an honest relationship is worth one hundred sales.*

Your integrity will always be remembered longer than your product.

Jesus was honest.

Prayer

Father, I ask You to help me develop and maintain a standard of truth and integrity. Strengthen me as I strive to be more like Jesus — sincere, honest, and trustworthy. Thank You that You will uphold me as I reach for Your standards. In Jesus' name, amen.

Questions

What are some examples you have seen or experienced when the truth paid off?

How would you handle a situation in which you gave someone the wrong information by mistake, but correcting it could cost you a sale or threaten your job?

Jesus Went Where
The People Were

"For, brethren, ye have been called unto liberty; only use not liberty for an occasion to the flesh, but by love serve one another."

GALATIANS 5:13

Somebody needs you.

Go find them. Activate yourself. Move toward neighbors. Move toward the members of your family. Get on the telephone. Go ahead, write that brief note to that close friend. You may be shy, timid, and even feel inadequate, but you will not succeed in life unless you are connected to people.

Success involves people. People who enable you to succeed may not always come to you. In fact, they rarely do. *You must go to them.*

Why do you think there are newspaper machines on every corner and soft drink machines on every floor of a hotel?

Successful people are accessible.

You will never possess what you are unwilling to pursue.

Jesus knew this. He did not set up a throne in the middle of each city and say, "This is my palace. This is the only place you can see Me." He went to the marketplace. He went to the boats of fishermen. He went to the synagogue. He went to the homes of the people. He went everywhere. He "went through the towns, preaching the gospel, and healing every where" (Luke 9:6).

WISDOM KEY
You Will Never Possess What You Are Unwilling To Pursue.

Jesus was reachable.

What is keeping you from reaching out toward others? Is it an inward fear or dread that you may be rejected or turned down? Are you intimidated in some way? There is something far more important than rejection: *Your dreams and goals.*

Successful people are reachers. They dread rejection, but they believe their goal is worth it.

Leadership Secret 4

Jesus left comfort. He left the presence of angels and His heavenly Father. He willingly walked into an atmosphere that was unholy and imperfect. He stepped out of a magnificent and perfect kingdom into a world that was confused, stained, and deadly. But, He walked *into* the lives of those who needed Him.

He went where the people were.

Your dream is connected to people. Lawyers need clients. Doctors need patients. Singers need musicians. Salespeople need customers.

Jesus went where people were hurting. He went to the lame, the blind, the poor, the wealthy. He talked to the learned, the ignorant, the hungry, the thirsty.

Start your "People-List" today. There are two kinds of people in your life: 1) Those who *already* know that you have something they need, and 2) those who do not yet know you have something they need.

Your "People-List" may include your relatives, neighbors, newspaper carrier, gardener, dentist, manicurist, hairdresser, landlord, doctor, or lawyer.

There is a *Law of Relationship* that says every person is merely four people away from any other human on earth. Think of it! This simply means that you know Bill, who knows Judy, who knows Charles, who knows anyone else you would ever want to know. *You are already networked with the entire world.*

You simply have to get out of your house. Get out of your car. Go to the door. Reach for your telephone.

Success always begins somewhere.

Success always begins at some moment.

Success always begins with someone.

You must go where people are.

Jesus did.

Prayer

Lord, I praise You for Your magnificent creation of men and women! I ask that You help me to reach out to others around me with boldness and confidence, as never before. I know that You have given me a plan and opportunity to reach people and succeed with them. In Jesus' name, amen.

Questions

What step will you take in the next two weeks to get to know one business contact or associate better?

What organization will you visit in the next 30 days to network with a larger group of people?

What special skill, talent, or pertinent information will you share with one person this week to help them grow?

Jesus Took Time To Rest

"And on the seventh day God ended his work which he had made; and he rested on the seventh day from all his work which he had made."

GENESIS 2:2

Fatigue can be costly.

One notable president of the United States knew this. He absolutely refused to make any major decisions after 4:00 in the afternoon. He knew that *a tired mind rarely makes good decisions.*

One bad decision can create countless tragedies.

Rest and recreation are not a sin. Rest time is *repair* time. It is *not* a loss of productivity. It is time for *renewing*. It is *receiving time*. It helps *release* your potential.

Jesus was an action man, a people person. He produced. He healed. He preached and taught. He walked among the people. *But, He also knew the necessity of rest and relaxation.* "Come ye yourselves apart into a desert place, and rest a while" (Mark 6:31).

Think about this. Every day Jesus faced hundreds of the sick and afflicted who screamed for His attention. Many were demon possessed. Mothers reached for Him. Fathers asked Him to pray for their children. Children did not want to leave His presence.

But Jesus *separated* Himself...*to receive.*

He knew He could only give away that which He possessed. Work time is *giving.* Rest time is *receiving.* You must have both.

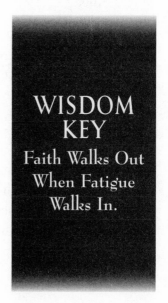

WISDOM KEY
Faith Walks Out When Fatigue Walks In.

God created the earth in six days, but He took the time to *rest* on the seventh day. He set an example for us. *Jesus did the same thing.*

Jesus understood the balance of rest and work, which might be the reason He was able to accomplish so much in three and one-half years.

Life is demanding. People are demanding. In fact, the more you succeed, the more people will demand of you.

Rebuilding yourself will require your attention.

Work hard, but play just as enthusiastically. *Schedule it.* Take one day a week off completely. Totally relax. Focus on something completely different than your job. Your mind will think clearer. You will make better decisions. You will see life through different eyes. You will accomplish far more in less time.

Stop your frantic push for success. Take time to *taste the present.* The fires of desire will *always* rage within you. You must dominate that rage and focus it. *Learn to rest.*

Jesus did.

Prayer

Lord, teach me how to rest. Show me how I can turn towards You and refresh and rejuvenate myself. I know that without rest, I cannot accomplish the goals and desires that You have placed within me. Thank You for Your rest! In Jesus' name, amen.

Questions

How often do you actually schedule rest and relaxation time?

What do you do to rest your mind at work? At home?

If you had one full day all to yourself, what would you do?

Jesus Took Time
To Plan

"Through skillful and godly Wisdom is a house [a life, a home, a family] built, and by understanding it is established [on a sound and good foundation]. And by knowledge shall the chambers [of its every area] be filled with all precious and pleasant riches."

PROVERBS 24:3,4 AMP

Champions plan.

Planning is the starting point for any dream or goal that you possess.

What is a plan? A plan is *a written list of arranged actions* necessary to achieve your desired goal. "Write the vision, and make it plain upon tables, that he may run that readeth it" (Habakkuk 2:2).

Jesus planned your future. "In my Father's house are many mansions: if it were not so, I would have told you. I go to prepare a place for you" (John 14:2).

Think for a moment. God scheduled the birth, the crucifixion, and resurrection of His Son before the foundation of the earth. "And all that dwell upon the earth shall worship him, whose names are not written in the book of life of the Lamb slain from the foundation of the world" (Revelation 13:8).

I think it is quite fascinating that God would schedule a meal, the marriage supper, six thousand years ahead of time! "Blessed are they which are called unto the marriage supper of the Lamb" (Revelation 19:9).

God always honored men who planned.

Noah *planned* the building of the ark. Solomon, the wisest man who ever lived on earth, *took time to plan* the building of the temple. Moses,

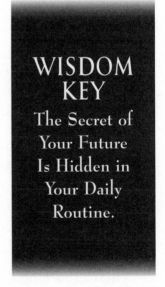

WISDOM KEY

The Secret of Your Future Is Hidden in Your Daily Routine.

the great deliverer who brought the Israelites out of Egypt, *took time to plan* the tabernacle.

Your Bible is the *plan of God* for you, the world, and eternity. It is the undeniable proof that God thinks ahead. Most of the Bible is prophecy, a description of the future before it ever occurs.

Jesus taught, "For which of you, intending to build a tower, sitteth not down first, and counteth the cost, whether he have sufficient to finish it? Lest haply, after he hath laid the foundation, and is not able to finish it, all that behold it begin to mock him, saying, This man began to build, and was not able to finish. Or what king, going to make war against another king, sitteth not down first, and consulteth whether he be able with ten thousand to meet him that cometh against him with twenty thousand?" (Luke 14:28-31).

Make a list of things to do every day of your life. Write six things you want to accomplish that day. Focus your total attention on each task. Assign each task to a specific time. (If you cannot plan events for twenty-four hours in your life, what makes you think you will accomplish your desires for the next twenty-four years?)

Think of each hour as an employee. *Delegate a specific assignment to each hour.* What do you want to accomplish between 7:00 a.m. and 8:00 a.m.? Who should you telephone today?

Write out your plan clearly on a sheet of paper. *Successes are usually scheduled events.* Failures are not.

Planning is laborious. It is tedious. It is meticulous. It is grilling, demanding, and exhausting. In my personal opinion, detailed planning is really never fun. *But, sometimes you have to do something you hate to create something you love.*

Why do people avoid planning? Some avoid it because it is time consuming. They are so busy "mopping up the water" that they do not take the time to "turn off the faucet!"

The secret of your future is hidden in your daily routine.

Planning is the starting point for any dream or goal that you possess.

Even ants think ahead. "Go to the ant, thou sluggard; consider her ways, and be wise: Which having no guide, overseer, or ruler, provideth her meat in the summer, and gathereth her food in the harvest" (Proverbs 6:6-8).

Jesus had a plan.

Prayer

Father, I thank You for giving me the ability to plan. I ask that You give me wisdom in ordering my daily routine so that it allows me to get the most out of every hour. In Jesus' name I pray, amen.

Questions

What is the biggest obstacle you face in being a more consistent planner?

How will you overcome this obstacle for the next 21 days?

Jesus Knew He Did Not Have To Close Every Sale To Be A Success

---

"And let us not be weary in well doing: for in due season we shall reap, if we faint not."

GALATIANS 6:9

"No" simply means to "ask again."

Stop for a moment. Review your past experiences. You encountered rejection when you were a child. Some of your schoolmates may not have liked you. But, you made it anyway, didn't you?

Rejection is not fatal. It is merely someone's opinion.

Jesus experienced more rejection than any human who ever lived on earth. He was born in a stable. He was born as an outcast in society. Even today, television talk show hosts belittle and make fun of Him and those who follow Him. The name of Jesus is used daily as a curse word by millions. His own people rejected Him.

"He came unto his own, and his own received him not" (John 1:11).

Did He quit? When Judas betrayed Him, did He allow Himself to become demoralized? No. *Jesus knew that He did not have to close every sale to be a success.* He went on to the others, those who discerned His value. "But as many as received him, to them gave he power to become the sons of God, even to them that believe on his name" (John 1:12). He knew His *worth.* He knew His *product.*

> **WISDOM KEY**
>
> Sometimes You Have To Do Things You Hate To Create Something You Love.

He knew that critics died, but His plan was eternal.

Jesus was willing to experience a *season of pain* to create an *eternity of gain. Some things last longer than rejection* — your goals and dreams.

Move beyond your scars. Not everyone will celebrate you. Not everyone will welcome your future.

Someone needs what you have. Your contribution is an absolute necessity for their success. Discern it.

Pharisees rejected Jesus. The religious sect called Sadducees rejected Him. Religious leaders despised Him. Those who should have recognized His worth wanted to destroy Him.

Jesus risked rejection to become the golden link between man and God.

Babe Ruth was famous for many years as the home run king in baseball history. Many people have never realized that he had more strikeouts than any other batter! They have not remembered his losses at bat. They merely remember his successes. He was willing to risk a strikeout to hit that home run.

Most great salespeople say that knowing that fourteen out of fifteen people will say no merely inspires them to hurry and make their presentations to as many as possible, to reach that one who will accept.

Jesus taught His disciples how to handle rejection. "And whosoever shall not receive you, nor hear your words, when ye depart out of that house or city, shake off the dust of your feet" (Matthew 10:14).

Climb out of your recliner! Make that telephone call. Write that letter.

Sooner or later you will succeed.

Jesus knew this.

Prayer

Lord, I thank You for Your faithfulness and reassurance in all times. Thank You for teaching me that sometimes I must be willing to experience a season of pain in order to receive a season of gain. You have given me the grace to do that which I do not like to do in order to achieve what I want. In Jesus' name, amen.

Questions

How have you successfully overcome an objection from a customer on a sale or the rejection of a new idea or proposal?

What two specific steps will you take to change the way you respond when someone says, "No" in the future?

Jesus Had Something Others Needed

"And the whole multitude sought to touch him: for there went virtue out of him, and healed them all."

LUKE 6:19

You were created to change somebody.

Every person you meet today is trying to *change* their life in some way. They desire excellence. They want *financial freedom*. They want their *health* to improve. They hate loneliness. You may not be sent to everyone, but you are definitely sent to someone.

You may not be qualified to help every person you meet. *But, somebody needs something you possess.* It may be your warmth, your love, your gifts, or a special opportunity you can provide them.

Jesus understood this. He knew that He could *change* people for *good*. He possessed something that could eliminate sorrow and heartache from their life. He was a *Restorer.* He was a *Repairer.* "The thief cometh not, but for to steal, and to kill, and to destroy: I am come that they might have life, and that they might have it more abundantly" (John 10:10). Jesus understood the insatiable appetite for self-improvement and excellence.

There are four kinds of people in your life: those who add, subtract, divide, or multiply. Every relationship will affect you — for good or bad. *Those who do not increase you inevitably will decrease you.* "He that walketh with wise men shall be wise: but a companion of fools shall be destroyed" (Proverbs 13:20). *Each relationship nurtures a strength or a weakness within you.*

> ## WISDOM KEY
> You Can Only Conquer Your Past By Focusing On Your Future.

Thousands of people want to *change.* They just don't know *how* to change. Every alcoholic hates his bondage. Most smokers long to quit. Drug addicts sit for hours wondering how they can break their chains of bondage.

42

Jesus looked for people in trouble. That's why He told His disciples that He needed to go through Samaria, where He met a woman with five marriages that had failed. He talked. She listened. He changed her life so permanently, she went back into the city proclaiming the influence of Jesus in her life. *She conquered her past by focusing on her future.*

"But whosoever drinketh of the water that I shall give him shall never thirst; but the water that I shall give him shall be in him a well of water springing up into everlasting life" (John 4:14). Jesus was water to the *thirsty*. He was bread to the *hungry*. He was a road map to the *lost*. He was a companion to the *lonely*.

Stop for a moment. What are your own greatest gifts? What is the *center of your expertise?* Are you a *good listener?* A good *speaker?* Whatever your gift is, that is what God will use to bless others through you.

Joseph had the ability to interpret dreams. Ruth took care of Naomi.

Your gift may not be needed by everybody, but it is definitely needed by *somebody*. Who needs your gift? What is your gift? Whose life are you capable of improving today? Whose income could you improve? Whose peace of mind could you affect?

You are capable of motivating *somebody*. Maybe you can provide a climate or atmosphere that unlocks the creativity of another. People want to succeed. People want to *improve*.

Someone has been waiting for you for a lifetime. They are worth pursuing. You are the golden thread missing in their life.

People want to *change*.

Jesus knew this.

Prayer

Thank You, Father, that You have placed within me a gift that is needed by someone in the world today. In Jesus' strength, I have been able to overcome my past by focusing on my gift and its possibilities. You have created me for a purpose. Help me to find those who need me the most. In Jesus' name I pray, amen.

Questions

How have you changed the life of someone in the past month?

What motivational techniques have you found to be the most effective in unlocking the creativity in others?

What special gift do you have that you find yourself frequently giving to others?

Jesus Was Concerned About People's Finances

"But my God shall supply all your need according to his riches in glory by Christ Jesus."

PHILIPPIANS 4:19

Money is a reward.

Money is what you receive *when you help someone else achieve their goal.*

Payday is simply reward day. You are rewarded for spending your best hours of each day, your energy, and knowledge helping your boss reach specific goals. They paid you for this!

Money is very important. You cannot live in your home without it. You cannot provide for your family without it. Your automobile costs money. Your clothes cost money. Most marriage counselors observe that the number one cause of divorce is financial conflict.

45

Jesus recognized the importance of money.

Some think Jesus was a wandering nomad who wore a dirty robe and sandals and lived off scraps of food in the villages He visited. To the contrary, He had twelve men who handled His business. One was the treasurer. (John 13:29).

Jesus did not want you to worry about finances. "Therefore I say unto you, Take no thought for your life, what ye shall eat, or what ye shall drink; nor yet for your body, what ye shall put on. Is not the life more than meat, and the body than raiment? Behold the fowls of the air: for they sow not, neither do they reap, nor gather into barns; yet your heavenly Father feedeth them. Are ye not much better than they?" (Matthew 6:25,26).

Jesus knew that God loved to give people good things. "Every good gift and every perfect gift is from above, and cometh down from the Father" (James 1:17).

Money is a fact of life. It is necessary. You need it. Money is on God's mind. It is taught about in the Word of God. In fact, 20 percent of Jesus' teaching and conversation was about money and finances.

God loves to see His people prosper. "Let the Lord be magnified, which hath pleasure in the prosperity of his servant" (Psalm 35:27).

God wants to reveal ways for you to profit and succeed financially. "I am the Lord thy God which teacheth thee to profit" (Isaiah 48:17).

Jesus showed people *how to get ahead financially* through His parables about using their gifts and wisely investing what He has given them. (Matthew 25:14-29).

Your future starts with whatever is in your hand today. Nothing is too little to multiply. Everything is *reproductive.* Everyone has received something from God which is capable of reproducing.

Jesus showed people that God was their true source of everything. (Matthew 6:31-34).

Jesus taught that giving was one of the ways to multiply what He has given you. "Give, and it shall be given unto you; good measure, pressed down, and shaken together, and running over, shall men give into your bosom. For with the same measure that ye mete withal it shall be measured to you again" (Luke 6:38).

WISDOM
KEY
Your Future
Begins With
Whatever Is In
Your Hands
Today.

Jesus taught how to unlock the promise of a 100-fold return. "There is no man that hath left house, or brethren, or sisters, or father, or mother, or wife, or children, or lands, for my sake, and the gospels, But he shall receive an hundredfold now in this time, houses, and brethren, and sisters, and mothers, and children, and lands, with persecutions; and in the world to come eternal life" (Mark 10:29,30).

Jesus taught that you could give your way out of trouble. "Give, and it will be given to you. A good measure, pressed down, and shaken together and running over, will be poured into your lap. For with the measure you use, it will be measured to you" (Luke 6:38 NIV).

Jesus taught fishermen where to drop their nets to catch fish (Luke 5:1-11). Notice these incredible secrets: 1) Jesus visited people *where* they worked. 2) Jesus was so interested in their work that He instructed them as to the right time to drop their fishing nets to catch fish. 3) The disciples had enough confidence in Jesus' knowledge that they went ahead and dropped their nets again, in total obedience. 4) They caught more fish than they had ever caught, so much that their net broke. 5) Their success was so remarkable they had to have partners to help them pull in the fish. 6) When the disciples saw the incredible knowledge and concern and results of following Jesus' instructions, they realized how sinful they were, how limited they were. 7) They brought their ships to land and decided to totally follow Jesus and His teachings.

Jesus took the time to show His disciples where to get money to pay their taxes. "Go thou to the sea, and cast an hook, and take up the fish that first cometh up; and when thou hast opened his mouth, thou shalt find a piece of money: that take, and give unto them for me and thee" (Matthew 17:27).

These are the facts: Jesus showed people *where* money could be found. He *motivated* them to try again and consider options and changes. He focused their mind on their *true source*, the heavenly Father. He encouraged them to make *spiritual* matters a priority. Then He encouraged them to look at their giving *as a seed given in faith to reap the promise of a 100-fold harvest.* He encouraged them *to expect a harvest* from everything they sowed into God's work by helping set others free.

> *Everyone has received something from God which is capable of reproducing.*

If there is one thing more exciting than discovering financial freedom God's way, it is helping others discover His plan for financial freedom too.

Jesus did.

Prayer

Father, I trust You and rely upon You as the source for my every financial need. Help me to fully grasp that the key to receiving finances is in sowing finances as You direct, no matter the amount. Please teach me how I can also show others how to discover financial freedom. In Jesus' name, amen.

Questions

What keys of wisdom has the Lord revealed to you about financial planning in your life? How can you share these nuggets with others?

How consistently do you tithe and give offerings to the work of the Lord?

What blessings have you received as a result of your sowing?

Jesus Was Willing To Go Where He Had Never Been Before

"Also I heard the voice of the Lord, saying, Whom shall I send, and who will go for us? Then said I, Here am I; send me."

ISAIAH 6:8

Geography makes a difference.

Pineapples do well in Hawaii. They do not do very well in Alaska. *Atmosphere matters.* The climate is important for any seed to grow.

You, too, are a seed. Your business and your product are like seeds. However, you may need to change locations and situations to unlock the full potential of your success.

Success requires people. You will never succeed without networking with many different kinds of people. They may

51

not be easily accessible. You may have to leave the comforts of your home or office to reach them and achieve extraordinary success.

Recently I was amazed by what I saw in the life of Jesus. He was constantly in *movement*, constantly *changing* locations.

"He was come down from the mountain" (Matthew 8:1). "He entered into Capernaum" (8:5). "[He]...was come into Peter's house" (8:14). "He was entered into a ship" (8:23). "And when he was come to the other side into the country of the Gergesenes..." (8:28).

> ## WISDOM KEY
> You Must Be Willing To Go Where You Have Never Been, To Create Something You Have Never Had.

Jesus was constantly arising, departing, and going to new places. He sought to be around new people. He discussed His teaching with many types of people of varied backgrounds.

Some people will not come to where you are. You have to go to their home, their town, and their environment.

Once, Jesus told His disciples to go to the upper room. They were to tarry there until they received the marvelous experience of the Holy Spirit. He told five hundred this. Three hundred eighty disobeyed Him. Even after they had observed His resurrection and His miracle life, only one hundred twenty out of the five hundred actually followed His instruction. But those who were willing to go to a different place — the Upper Room — received the marvelous outpouring of the Holy Spirit.

Abraham, the patriarch of the Israelites, had to make *geographical changes* before his success was birthed. (Genesis 12:1,2.)

Joseph found his incredible success in *another country*, Egypt.

Ruth willingly left her heathen family in Moab and went to Bethlehem with Naomi. There she met Boaz, a financial giant of the community, and married him.

It is normal to move toward those who are easily accessible.

Sometimes you have to go somewhere you have never been before you taste the extraordinary success that you want to experience.

Jesus did.

Prayer

Father, I know that You have a plan for me. I ask that You help me to be willing to go where I have never been before so You can help me create the success I have never experienced before. In Jesus' name, amen.

Questions

What benefits have you experienced by changing jobs, companies, or geographic locations?

How can you prepare yourself or help others to major on the opportunities and not the obstacles when faced with times of change?

Jesus Never Allowed What Others Said About Him To Change His Opinion Of Himself

---

"Blessed are ye, when men shall hate you, and when they shall separate you from their company, and shall reproach you, and cast out your name as evil, for the Son of man's sake. Rejoice ye in that day, and leap for joy: for, behold, your reward is great in heaven: for in the like manner did their fathers unto the prophets."

LUKE 6:22,23

Nobody really knows you.

Consider this for a moment. Almost everyone in your life is more preoccupied with themselves than you. Therefore, you know more about yourself than anyone who will ever meet you. Never forget this.

It is not what men say about you that really matters in life. *It is what you believe about yourself.*

Jesus was slandered. He was falsely accused. They said He was possessed with devils. Countless accusations were hurled like stones against Jesus every day of His life, but it never affected Him.

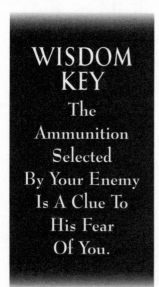

WISDOM KEY

The Ammunition Selected By Your Enemy Is A Clue To His Fear Of You.

Jesus knew what He was really about. He believed in Himself. He believed in His product. He knew His accusers were ignorant, unlearned, and arrogant. He knew they simply feared Him.

People always fight what they do not understand. *The mind will always resent what it cannot master.* Wars are fought because of ignorance and fear. Throughout human history, champions have had their names soiled and stained. Accusations and slanderous lies have come against great political leaders as well as ministers. This is life. Daniel was accused of breaking the law. Joseph was falsely accused of raping his employer's wife. Paul was accused of arousing mobs through hatred and division concerning the belief systems of religious people.

Jesus never begged anyone to believe in Him. He knew that *integrity cannot be proven, it must be discerned.*

He never wasted time with critics. He kept His attention on His goal. *He stayed focused.*

They accused Jesus of being filled with devils! He paid no attention. He simply continued to cast out devils. (Matthew 12:24.)

WISDOM KEY

Integrity
Cannot Be
Proved;
It Must Be
Discerned.

Jesus never strived to "look good." *He simply was good.* He did not labor to appear truthful. *He was truthful.* He never struggled to have a good reputation. *He had character.*

Every successful person wants to be loved and admired, but your enemies and critics will never leave your reputation unstained and untarnished. You must rise above that fact. You must never allow what others say about you to change your personal opinion of yourself. *Never.*

Jesus did not.

Prayer

I pray, Lord, that I will not waste time concerning myself with what others say about me. I thank You for the strength and faithfulness to not fall into an appearance of good or integrity, but to be a person of goodness, truth, and character. In Jesus' name, amen.

Questions

Did you respond positively or react negatively the last time someone said something negative or untrue about you?

If you could go back and replay the scene again, what would you do differently?

List three examples of people who have risen above the circumstances when they have been lied about or rejected. What did they do to respond positively?

Jesus Understood Timing And Preparation

"By faith Noah, being warned of God of things not seen as yet, moved with fear, prepared an ark to the saving of his house."

HEBREWS 11:7

Champions never hurry.

The quality of preparation determines the quality of performance.

Great concert pianists invest hundreds of hours of practice before a concert. They know that the quality of those many grueling hours of practice will prepare them for their greatest performance. The world champion heavyweight boxer knows he cannot get into the ring with his opponent without preparing first. It would be too late. For many weeks before the great fight, he toils in his morning workout, running, and exercise program.

Champions do not *become* champions in the ring. They are merely *recognized* in the ring. Their *becoming* happens in their *daily routine*.

Jesus never hurried.

Jesus did not begin His earthly ministry until He was thirty years old. His ministry was a short three- and one-half years.

His preparation time was thirty years.

WISDOM KEY

Every Season Has A Product.

Jesus was very sensitive about timing. When His mother told Him that the people had run out of wine at the marriage of Cana, He replied, "Woman, what have I to do with thee? mine hour is not yet come" (John 2:4). Obviously, God was planning a public introduction of Jesus' ministry, but Jesus saw a need and responded to the faith Mary expressed when she said, "Whatsoever he saith unto you, do it" (John 2:5).

Something *good* is happening every moment of your life. *Something* is growing bigger. It may be the seed of patience or a new friendship just birthed. It may also be that the weaknesses of your plans are being revealed. Whatever it is, each season is producing some specific result from your efforts.

Look for the reward of the present season, regardless of whether it appears to be a success or a failure. Preparation chapters in your life are not delays in your future success. Each chapter and season has a benefit and a product, if you will look for them.

Several years ago, a friend of mine had just entered a business. He was so excited about its remarkable potential. However, he did not want to spend time learning how to present the plan to others. He felt it was just "too detailed." As I watched him stumble over and over in his conversations with others, I finally said, "Learn the business. Study the products. Take time to learn the details. *If you will take the time to prepare, your presentation will have believability.* The people will have confidence in becoming a part of your business. You may not learn all the details the first night you hear them, but don't worry; set aside a few hours each week to begin to prepare your presentation."

Preparation time is never wasted time.

It will take time to know your business. It will take time to know your product. It will take time to develop a list of customers and clients.

Think about the life of Jesus. He saw hundreds around Him because of sickness and disease, but His time had not come. He saw thousands warped with the traditions and legalism of religious systems, but He knew His Father was growing Him up. "And Jesus increased in wisdom and stature, and in favour with God and man" (Luke 2:52). Jesus was willing to wait.

He *prepared* Himself.

Prayer

Father, thank You for teaching me that champions aren't made but they are recognized. With Your strength, I can make time my servant and prepare with excellence so that my performance reflects excellence. In Jesus' name, amen.

Questions

In what two ways can you prepare yourself to be more effective in your work during the next 30 days?

Consider an example when you weren't sensitive to proper timing in an important situation. What did you learn to do differently from that episode?

Jesus Developed A Passion For His Goals

"And whatsoever ye do, do it heartily, as to the Lord, and not unto men."

COLOSSIANS 3:23

Passion is power.

You will never have significant success with anything *until it becomes an obsession with you.* An obsession is when something *consumes* your thoughts and time.

You will only be remembered in life for your obsession. Henry Ford, the automobile. Thomas Edison, inventions. Billy Graham, evangelism. Oral Roberts, healing. The Wright brothers, the airplane.

Jesus had a passion for His mission and goal in life. "For the Son of man is come to seek and to save that which was lost" (Luke 19:10). "How God anointed Jesus of Nazareth with the Holy Ghost and with power: who went about doing good, and healing all that were oppressed of the devil; for God was with him" (Acts 10:38).

Jesus focused on doing the exact instructions of His heavenly Father. He healed the sick. He noticed the lonely. He came to make people successful, to restore and repair their life to full fellowship with His Father.

Jesus' obsession took Him to the cross. It took Him to the crucifixion. Eight inches of thorns were crushed into His brow. A spear punctured His side. Spikes were driven into His hands. Thirty-nine stripes of a whip tore His back to shreds. One commentary states that four hundred soldiers spit on His body. His beard was ripped off His face. But He was *obsessed with the salvation of mankind.*

And He succeeded.

You may start small. You may start with very little. But, if what you love begins to consume your mind, your thoughts, your conversation, your schedule — look for extraordinary success.

> **WISDOM KEY**
> You Will Only Have Significant Success With Something That Is An Obsession.

Do you dread going to work every morning? Do you anxiously look at the clock toward closing time each afternoon? Is your mind wandering throughout the day toward other places or things you would love to be doing? Then you will probably not have much success at what you are doing.

Find something that consumes you, something that is worthy of building your entire life around. Consider it.

Jesus did.

Prayer

Father, I know that unless I set my heart upon a goal, I will not accomplish it. I ask that You give me the diligence and wisdom to turn Your goal into my strongest desire. I will only get out of something what I have put in it. In Jesus' name, amen.

Questions

What is one special desire you have concerning your future?

On a score of one to ten, how would you measure your level of passion for that desire to be fulfilled?

What will you do in the next 30 days to put a plan into action to turn that desire into reality?

Jesus Respected Authority

"Servants, be obedient to them that are your masters according to the flesh, with fear and trembling, in singleness of your heart, as unto Christ; Not with eyeservice, as menpleasers; but as the servants of Christ, doing the will of God from the heart."

EPHESIANS 6:5,6

Authority creates order.

Imagine a nation without a leader. A workplace without a boss. An army without a general. Authority creates order, *the accurate arrangement of things.* That is why you do not park your car in your bathroom! You do not eat your meals in the garage! There is a time and a place for everything.

Leadership Secret 14

Respect those in authority over you. Your success is affected by it. Honor those who have lived before you. They possess a wealth of knowledge. Listen. Learn. Observe them.

Mentorship is the Master Key to extraordinary success.

Jesus understood this. He was the Son of God. He knew more than any other human on earth. Yet, He honored the authority of the Roman government. When people came to Him, questioning His opinion of paying taxes to Caesar, He answered, "Render to Caesar the things that are Caesar's, and to God the things that are God's" (Mark 12:17).

Are you speaking words of doubt about your own organization? Are you belittling or criticizing those in authority over you? Stop it now! True, those in authority may not be perfect. They make mistakes. (Maybe that's why they can tolerate you! If they were perfect, they might not want to communicate with you either!)

WISDOM KEY
You Will Never Be Promoted Until You Become Over-Qualified For Your Present Position.

If you are rebelling against every instruction given to you, then do not complain when those around you begin to rebel against your words and opinions. Learn to honor and respect those in authority over you.

Jesus did.

Prayer

Father, I know that respect for authority comes straight from Your Word. I ask that You remind me at every turn that my success depends largely upon my respect and attitude towards those in leadership over me. I pray You will be with them and honor them in all they do. In Jesus' name, amen.

Questions

How often do you pray for those in authority over you?

What will you do in the next seven days to show honor and appreciation to one person who is in authority over you?

Jesus Never Discriminated

"These things also belong to the wise.
It is not good to have respect of persons
in judgment."

PROVERBS 24:23

Treat people right.

Some years ago, Elvis Presley did a concert in Indianapolis, Indiana. One of my close friends, a deputy sheriff in Indianapolis, was in charge of security backstage. He noticed that a man dressed in an old windbreaker jacket was shuffling around, as if he was some bum off the street. As my friend prepared to evict him from the building, someone stopped him and said, "That man is Colonel Parker, the manager of Elvis Presley." He was shocked and stunned. He had misjudged the man because of his appearance.

Stop prejudging people. Your first impression is always limited. It is possibly very wrong. *Only fools make permanent decisions without knowledge.* Never assume your intuition or perception is always correct.

Your success in business will be affected by prejudice, fear, and any discrimination you allow.

Jesus never discriminated because of someone's race, sex, financial status, or appearance.

He was comfortable in the presence of fishermen or the tax collectors of His day. He was at ease with men and women, the rich and the poor.

WISDOM KEY
Nobody Is Ever As They First Appear.

Jesus knew that every person contains potential. He never eliminated someone just because of their past. Born of a mother who conceived Him as a virgin, He knew what it meant to have a questionable background. He rose above it.

Jesus broke tradition. When the Samaritans were considered a lower class of people and Jews would not even talk to them, Jesus did. In fact, He took time with the Samaritan woman at the well, discussing her entire life and *how He could change it*.

Peter said it this way, "Of a truth I perceive that God is no respecter of persons" (Acts 10:34).

James wrote it this way, "For if there come unto your assembly a man with a gold ring, in goodly apparel, and there come in also a poor man in vile raiment; And ye have respect to him that weareth the gay clothing, and say unto him, Sit thou here in a good place; and say to the poor, Stand thou there, or sit here under my footstool: Are ye not then partial in yourselves, and are become judges of evil thoughts?" (James 2:2-4).

Never eliminate anyone from the chain of your success.

Jesus refused to discriminate.

Prayer

Father, I know that You have created all people and that they are equal in Your sight. Thank You for giving me the wisdom not to condemn or prejudge someone solely on first impressions. I trust in Your patience and discernment, that

You will reveal true character and intentions to me, and I will not rely simply on appearance. In Jesus' name, amen.

Questions

What percentage of your time do you spend with people who dress, act, and do things just like you do?

What can you do to support and include men and women with diversified talents, experience levels, backgrounds, and cultures in your business group?

Jesus Offered Incentives

"And, behold, I come quickly; and my reward is with me, to give every man according as his work shall be."

REVELATION 22:12

Reward those who help you succeed.

People are motivated by two forces: pain or pleasure, fear or reward, loss or gain.

For example, you may ask your son to mow the lawn. He sulks and complains, "But Daddy, I don't really want to mow the lawn today. I want to go play with my friends."

You have two ways to motivate him: pain or pleasure, fear or incentive, loss or gain. For instance you may say, "Then son, bend over. I will have to discipline you with the rod." That is the *pain* motivation.

Or, you may use the *reward system.* "Son, I know you do not feel like doing it, but if you do it, I will pay you $10." That is *incentive.* Reward. Gain.

Jesus used both methods to motivate.

Jesus used fear motivation on the Pharisees who ridiculed Him. He described to them how the rich man went to hell and was "tormented in this flame" (Luke 16:24).

However, when Jesus was talking to His disciples, He used *rewards and incentives* to motivate them. "In my Father's house are many mansions: if it were not so, I would have told you. I go to prepare a place for you" (John 14:2).

> ## WISDOM KEY
> You Will Always Move Toward Anyone Who Increases You and Away From Anyone Who Decreases You.

You are created with a desire to *increase. Decrease is unnatural.* Remember, every person you meet today has an *appetite for increase.* They want to be benefited. There is nothing wrong with that. There is a God-given command on the inside of each person to become more, *to multiply.* (Genesis 1:28.)

Carefully examine the benefits you offer to others. Who *needs* your product? *Why* do they need it? What *problem* will your product *solve in their life?* What do you offer others *that they cannot find anywhere else?*

Study the incentives of your present business. Know them "like the palm of your hand."

People never buy your product for the reasons you sell it. They buy products *for what it will do for them.*

David asked what rewards would come to him if he killed the giant Goliath. He was told he would never have to pay taxes again, and he would be able to marry the king's daughter. He took five stones and killed the giant. *He had motivation. He had an incentive.*

> *Reward those who help you succeed.*

People do things for different reasons. Interview people. Ask questions. Find out what their greatest needs are. Dig to discover what their greatest fears may be.

Remember, you are there to *solve a problem.* Take the time to show others "what is in it for them." Make sure they understand the rewards and benefits of conducting business with you.

Jesus did.

Prayer

Father, You have made me a problem-solver. My product is designed to solve other people's problems. You have created me to increase and help others avoid decrease, by helping them increase too. Thank You for this ability. In Jesus' name, amen.

Questions

Besides a paycheck, how do you reward those who help you succeed?

Keeping in mind that features tell and benefits sell, what are three benefits of your product or of doing business with you?

Jesus Overcame The Stigma Of A Questionable Background

"Brethren, I count not myself to have apprehended: but this one thing I do, forgetting those things which are behind, and reaching forth unto those things which are before, I press toward the mark for the prize of the high calling of God in Christ Jesus."

PHILIPPIANS 3:13,14

Your past is over.

Are you having self-doubts today? This is common. Some of the reasons you doubt may be a limited education, losing a close loved one when you were young, an alcoholic parent, or guilt over a serious mistake you made in your teenage years.

But whatever the reason, it is very important that you remember your past is over.

Never build your future around your past.

Jesus was born with a terrible stigma. His mother, Mary, was pregnant with Him before she ever married Joseph, her betrothed. The Bible says that they had not had a sexual relationship, but, "that which is conceived in her is of the Holy Ghost" (Matthew 1:20).

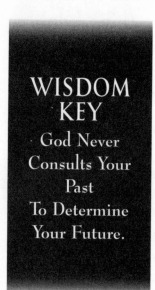

WISDOM KEY
God Never Consults Your Past To Determine Your Future.

Only two people in the world really knew that Mary was a virgin: God and Mary.

Undoubtedly, hundreds of people mocked and sneered at Joseph for marrying Mary.

Jesus grew up with this. He stepped out of a cesspool of human scorn. He clawed His way out of a pit of questions. He ignored the slanderous remarks. He knew the truth. He knew who He was and what He was about. It did not matter that others did not believe. *He chose to chart His own course.* The opinions of others did not matter.

Jesus never looked back. He never discussed the situation with anyone. There is not a single scripture in the entire Bible where He ever brought up His background or His limitations.

You too can move beyond the scars of yesterday. Stop talking about your limited education. Quit complaining that everyone in your family is poor. Stop repeating stories of those who failed you. Stop pointing your finger at the economy.

WISDOM KEY

Stop Looking At Where You Have Been And Start Looking At Where You Are Going.

Stop advertising your pain. Stop meditating on your flaws. Everyone has limitations. Each of us is handi-capped in some way: Physically. Emotionally. Mentally. Spiritually.

Concentrate on your *future*.

Jesus did.

Prayer

Thank You, Father, for Your Son who died on the cross and removed my past. You do not look at my past to determine my future. I know that if I rely upon You and concentrate on my future, my success is determined. In Jesus' name, amen.

Questions

What three specific qualities do you admire in someone who has overcome the stigma of a questionable background?

How have you applied these qualities in your own life?

How do you overcome self-doubt?

Jesus Never Wasted Time Answering Critics

"Go from the presence of a foolish man, when thou perceivest not in him the lips of knowledge."

PROVERBS 14:7

Critics are spectators, not players.

Critical people are usually disheartened people who have failed to reach a desired goal. Someone has said, "Criticism is the death gargle of a nonachiever."

There has never been a monument built to a critic.

Critical people are *disappointed* people. *Disillusioned* people. *Unfocused* people. They are hurting inside. They build their life trying to destroy others.

Move away from them.

Don't get me wrong, debate is a marvelous arena. Conflict unlocks my energy.

But, there is a place to present facts. There is a time for exchange of information. Constructive suggestions are always pursued by champions.

There is also a time *for silence.*

When Jesus was being ridiculed and prepared for His crucifixion, He was silent. "But Jesus held His peace" (Matthew 26:63). Jesus did not feel obligated to answer critics. He never wasted time on people who were obviously trying to trap Him. He responded to *hunger.* He responded to *thirst.* He responded to *seekers.*

WISDOM KEY

Never Spend
More Time On
A Critic
Than You
Would Give To
A Friend.

You owe nothing to a critic. "Speak not in the ears of a fool: for he will despise the wisdom of thy words" (Proverbs 23:9).

Criticism is deadly.

Correction is life.

Criticism is pointing out your flaws.

Correction is pointing out your potential.

Many years ago, I sat down at my kitchen table to reply to a critical letter from a lady. I toiled over my reply. I erased words and wrote new sentences. It took me over one hour of exhausting work to carefully carve out a decent response to her letter. I still wasn't satisfied with my answer to her. Suddenly, I began to laugh as a thought dawned. It hit me that I had never spent an entire hour writing a letter to my own mother, the dearest person in the world to me. I had never spent one hour writing to the woman who had carried me within her womb for nine months, provided comfort and food during my life, motivated me toward God and to learn to play the piano. I had not spent that much time on the most important person in my life. I was a fool to spend that much time on a critic.

Jesus ignored the critics.

Prayer

Lord, I know that the time I spend answering critics is time wasted. I ask that You give me the strength and maturity to rise above those who are critical and invest time in those whom I love and care for. In Jesus' name, amen.

Questions

How do you differentiate between constructive suggestions/correction and unproductive criticism?

What can you do to guard yourself from reacting to criticism?

Jesus Knew There Was A Right Time And A Wrong Time To Approach People

---

"See then that ye walk circumspectly, not as fools, but as wise, redeeming the time, because the days are evil. Wherefore be ye not unwise, but understanding what the will of the Lord is."

EPHESIANS 5:15-17

There is a time for everything.

There is a right time to approach people.

Suppose you want a raise. You want to let your boss know what you can do to be worth more to him. However, if you have just made a terrible mistake that cost the company $15,000.00, that is not the right time to approach him about your raise! If the company has just experienced incredible profits because of an idea you shared with your boss, that might be the proper climate and atmosphere to discuss it with him.

Jesus understood timing. He spent 30 years preparing for His ministry before He launched His first miracle. When His mother told Him that they had no wine at the wedding, Jesus responded to her, "Mine hour is not yet come" (John 2:4). Again, while His public ministry qualified for a proper introduction, Jesus honored the faith of His mother and turned water into wine.

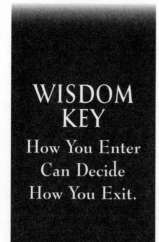

WISDOM KEY

How You Enter Can Decide How You Exit.

There is a time to ask for forgiveness. There is a time to be silent. There is a time to make presentations to people. There is a time to wait.

People are in different seasons of their lives. Moods change. Circumstances affect their decisions. *Be sensitive to this.*

It is a rare husband who can anticipate the moods and needs of his wife and respond appropriately. It is a brilliant teenager who knows and understands proper timing in discussing problems with his parents.

Jesus understood timing. When they caught the woman in the act of adultery, His reaction was unique. "And Jesus said unto her, 'Neither do I condemn thee: go, and sin no more'" (John 8:11).

He did not ignore her sin. He did not ignore the accusatory tone of the men wanting to trap her. He simply knew there was a proper time to do things. He did not dissect the woman's sin. He did not unravel the details of the adulterous act. He never dwelt on the past, but pointed to the future. There was a time for that.

"To every thing there is a season, and a time to every purpose under the heaven...He hath made everything beautiful in His time" (Ecclesiastes 3:1,11).

Your success depends on *timing*. Don't forget it! Whether you are selling to a customer or sitting at the discussion table with your boss, remain sensitive. Observe. Watch. Listen to the flow of information and what is going on.

Jesus did.

Prayer

Father, Your Word says that for each and every thing there is a season. I pray that You grant me the wisdom to recognize the proper timing for all that I do. Please bless me with the understanding that how I enter a situation can decide how I leave it. In Jesus' name, amen.

Questions

How often do you pray for the Lord's guidance about timing *before* you present new ideas or suggest a change in approach or procedure?

What key factors do you consider to determine the right timing to submit a business proposal?

Jesus Educated Those He Mentored

> "Give instruction to a wise man, and he will be yet wiser: teach a just man, and he will increase in learning."
>
> PROVERBS 9:9

You will always remember what you teach.

Someone has said that you don't learn anything when you talk; you only learn when you listen. That is inaccurate. Some of the greatest thoughts and ideas have surfaced while I was teaching others.

It is very important that you mentor someone. Train them. Teach them what you know — especially those over whom you have authority, any person who is carrying out an instruction for you, such as employees, children, and so on.

Successful businesses have employees who are informed, well trained, and confident about carrying out their instructions. This takes time. It takes energy. It takes great patience.

Every song needs a singer. Every achiever needs motivation. Every student needs a teacher.

Jesus was a master teacher. He taught thousands at a time. Sometimes He sat with His twelve disciples and fed information into them. He kept them motivated, influenced, and inspired.

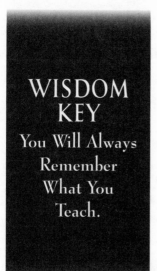

WISDOM
KEY
You Will Always
Remember
What You
Teach.

He taught them about prayer. (Matthew 26:36-46.) He taught them about heaven. (John 14:2-4.) He taught them about hell. (Luke 16:20-31.) He educated His staff on many topics, including His purpose, giving, and relationships.

Jesus taught in synagogues. (Luke 13:10.) He also taught in the villages. (Mark 6:6.)

Here is the point. None of us were born with great knowledge. You became what you are. You *discovered* what you know. It took time, energy, and learning.

Your staff will not know everything. They may not see what you see. They may not feel what you feel. They may not have discovered what you know.

You must invest time to nurture their vision, their product knowledge, and the rewards you want them to pursue.

> *No one was born with great knowledge. You become what you are. You discovered what you know.*

You need good people around you. You need *inspired* people around you. You need *informed* people around you. You may be their *only* source for information and motivation.

Jesus educated His staff. He constantly motivated the people He led by showing them the future of their present commitment.

Take the time to train others.

Jesus did.

Prayer

Father, just as Jesus educated His disciples, I choose to educate my staff. Thank You for revealing to me the most effective means of teaching and training those around me. I know that without a successor, there is no success. In Jesus' name, amen.

Questions

What significant achievements of your own do you attribute to someone who has taken time to teach and encourage you?

Who are you currently encouraging and teaching to be all they can be?

What are you doing to prepare someone to be your successor?

Jesus Refused To Be Discouraged When Others Misjudged His Motives

---

"The words of the wicked are to lie in wait for blood: but the mouth of the upright shall deliver them."

PROVERBS 12:6

Everyone has been misjudged.

When a minister speaks on giving, he risks being accused of greed. When he prays for the sick, he risks being called a fraud and a fake.

Your own family may misjudge your motives. Any person who carries out instructions for you may misjudge your actions.

Your boss might misread you. Customers may doubt your sincerity.

Don't be discouraged by that. Take the time to discuss your position with those who appear genuinely sincere. Do not waste your time and energy on those who are merely stirring up conflict.

Jesus was constantly misjudged by others. Pharisees accused Him of being possessed by evil spirits. "But when the Pharisees heard it, they said, 'This fellow doth not cast out devils, but by Beelzebub the Prince of the devils'" (Matthew 12:24).

WISDOM KEY

False Accusation Is The Last Stage Before Supernatural Promotion.

Let me make a few suggestions. When you speak to others, be concise. Be bold but very distinct in what you say. Do not leave room for misunderstanding.

Always be where you are. When you are in conversation with someone, totally focus on that conversation. Shut out everything else. When you totally focus on what you are saying and hearing, you do not have to reflect later on with regret about that conversation. This can prevent unnecessary misjudgment.

Every extraordinary achiever has been misjudged. People laughed over the thought of a horseless carriage. Others sneered when the telephone was invented.

Your success is on the other side of scorn and false accusations.

Jesus knew this.

Prayer

Father, thank You for redeeming situations in which others are critical of me or falsely accuse me. I rest in knowing that as I pattern myself after Jesus in ignoring my accusers, I will reach the other side of adversity — success. In Jesus' name, amen.

Questions

What specific scriptures are an encouragement to you when you face adversity? Have you memorized them?

How do you respond when someone misunderstands your motives?

How often do you meet with your staff and associates to keep them informed on projects, operations or anticipated changes?

Jesus Refused To Be Bitter When Others Were Disloyal Or Betrayed Him

"Finally, be ye all of one mind, having compassion one of another, love as brethren, be pitiful, be courteous: Not rendering evil for evil, or railing for railing: but contrariwise blessing; knowing that ye are thereunto called, that ye should inherit a blessing."

1 PETER 3:8,9

Bitterness is more devastating than betrayal.

Betrayal is external. Bitterness is internal. Betrayal is something that *others do to you*. Bitterness is something *you do to yourself*.

Thousands survive betrayal easily. Very few can survive the currents of bitterness. "Looking diligently lest any man fail of the grace of God; lest any root of bitterness springing up trouble you, and thereby many be defiled" (Hebrews 12:15).

Disloyalty is a product of an unthankful heart. Betrayal is usually the child of jealousy.

Everybody has experienced these tragic situations in their life. An unfaithful mate. An employee who slanders you behind your back. A boss who fires you without explanation. These things hurt. Deeply.

Jesus was at supper with His disciples. "And as they sat and did eat, Jesus said, "Verily I say unto you, One of you which eateth with me shall betray me" (Mark 14:18). When Jesus saw Judas was the one who would betray Him, He also saw something *more important* than the hurt and wounds of betrayal — the redemption of mankind!

Read Mark 14:43-50 and you will see one of the most demoralizing

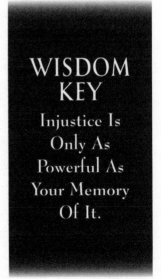

WISDOM KEY

Injustice Is Only As Powerful As Your Memory Of It.

experiences any human can experience. Judas betrayed Jesus with a kiss.

Yet, Jesus refused to be bitter.

Neither did He penalize Judas. Judas destroyed himself. Jesus did not disconnect from Peter, who denied Him. Peter cried out for mercy and forgiveness, and he was restored, becoming the great preacher on the Day of Pentecost.

"Let all bitterness, and wrath, and anger and clamor, and evil speaking, be put away from you, with all malice: And be ye kind one to another, tenderhearted, forgiving one another, even as God for Christ's sake hath forgiven you" (Ephesians 4:31,32).

Eliminate any words of bitterness in every conversation. Do not remind others of your experience, unless it is to teach and encourage them to rise above their own hurts.

Jesus saw the chapter beyond betrayal.

He refused to be bitter.

Prayer

Thank You, Lord, for removing any bitterness from my heart. I will be on guard against bitterness in the future. I will remember that when I am betrayed or judged unjustly, I can look past the hurt and see that bitterness is only a roadblock to success. In Jesus' name, amen.

Questions

How frequently do you revisit the pain of a past hurt?

What have you done to be sure no bitterness remains in your heart over that hurt?

How will you guard yourself against bitterness in the future?

Jesus Networked With People Of All Backgrounds

"The heart of the prudent getteth knowledge; and the ear of the wise seeketh knowledge."

PROVERBS 18:15

Greatness is everywhere.

People have different contributions. I believe you need different kinds of input into your life. Someone needs what you possess. You need something that they can contribute to you. You are the sum total of your experiences.

Personalities differ. Each person around you contains a different body of knowledge. It is up to you to "drop your pail in their well," and draw it out. "Where no counsel is, the people fall: but in the multitude of counsellors there is safety" (Proverbs 11:14).

Leadership Secret 23

Look at those who surrounded Jesus. A tax collector. A physician. Fishermen. A woman who had been possessed with seven devils.

Some were poor. Some were wealthy. Some were very energetic, while others were passive. Some were explosive like Peter. Others, like James, were logical.

Be willing to listen to others. Everyone sees through different eyes. They feel with different hearts. They hear through different ears. *Someone knows something that you should know.* You will not discover it until you take the time to stop and hear them out. *One piece of information can turn a failure into a success.* Great decisions are products of great thoughts.

Jesus networked.

Prayer

I realize, Lord, that Your creation is filled with many extraordinary and different people. Give me the wisdom and ability to recognize that who I spend my time with is time

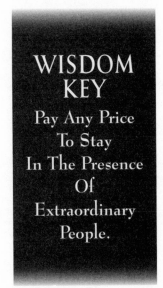

WISDOM KEY

Pay Any Price To Stay In The Presence Of Extraordinary People.

invested in my success and theirs. In Jesus' name, I rely upon You as my source. Amen.

Questions

How do you specifically plan ways to spend quality time with a variety of extraordinary people?

How do you record and store the important knowledge and experiences you glean from them so you can retrieve it later?

Jesus Resisted Temptation

"The Lord knoweth how to deliver the godly out of temptations."

2 PETER 2:9

Everybody is tempted.

Temptation is the presentation of evil. It is an opportunity to choose temporary pleasure rather than permanent gain.

You will experience many seasons during your life. During your teenage years, you may feel overwhelming currents of lust toward immorality. In the business world, you will be tempted to distort the truth, cheat on your taxes, or even "pocket extra money for yourself." Unfaithful mates are epidemic. Billboards boldly declare their invitation to alcohol. Drugs are on every corner. Cocaine appears to be an escape from the complexities of life.

Satan is a master artist.

Jesus experienced a relentless and persistent adversary, the Devil. It happened after He had fasted forty days and forty nights. His defense was quite simple: The written WORD OF GOD. I encourage you to read the entire account in Matthew 4:1-11.

The graveyard is full of people who failed to resist Satan. The prisons are overcrowded with people too weak to stand against him. Dreams crash daily on the rocks of temptation.

Move the ship of your life away from those rocks. Ask Samson and he will tell you, "One night of pleasure is not worth a lifetime of blindness."

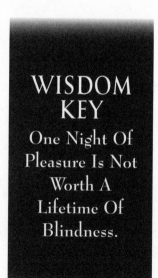

WISDOM KEY

One Night Of Pleasure Is Not Worth A Lifetime Of Blindness.

Fight Back.

Jesus did.

Prayer

Father, I know that when I am tempted, I must boldly stand upon the Word of God. With Your strength, I can resist evil and not sacrifice my future for the present. In Jesus' name, I have the conviction to do what is right. Amen.

Questions

In what specific areas of your life do you struggle with temptation?

How do you overcome these temptations, and what percentage of the time are you successful?

Have you identified and/or memorized any scriptures to help you overcome these specific areas of temptation in your life?

Jesus Made Decisions That Created A Desired Future Instead Of A Desired Present

---

"That ye be not slothful, but followers of them who through faith and patience inherit the promises."

HEBREWS 6:12

Decisions create events.

If you eat two slices of pecan pie every night, what will be the inevitable result? If you smoke two packs of cigarettes daily, what can you expect to happen? Everything you are presently doing will benefit your *present* or your *future*. The choice is yours.

You will make a lot of decisions today. Some of them will give you pleasure today, but the result of them tomorrow will make you miserable. Some of those decisions may make you a little uncomfortable today, but tomorrow you will be thrilled.

Tonight you will sit down at supper. Your mouth will water at the beautiful chocolate cake someone has prepared. You will make a decision about that chocolate cake. If you eat it, it will taste good for now. Tomorrow morning you will be unhappy with yourself for not refusing it. Look at that piece of cake and say, "I'm going to make a decision that *benefits my future*. I refuse it." That is the decision of a champion!

Jesus could have called ten thousand angels to deliver Him from the crucifixion. He was capable of coming down from the cross. But, He made the decision in the garden of Gethsemane that created an incredible future. *He was willing to go through a season of pain to create an eternity of gain.*

WISDOM KEY
Make Decisions That Will Create The Future You Desire.

"For our light affliction, which is but for a moment, worketh for us a far more exceeding and eternal weight of glory" (2 Corinthians 4:17).

Those who wait usually win. Those who refuse to wait usually lose. Patience is powerful. It is productive.

Reprogram your thinking to distance. Reprogram your life for endurance. Start thinking "long term" about your eating habits, your prayer life, and your friendships.

Jesus was a "long termer."

Prayer

In Jesus' name, I commit myself to thinking for the long term and not the short term. I know that each and every decision I make has an impact upon my future. Thank You, Father, for giving me the wisdom to make decisions that create my desired future. Amen.

Questions

How do you need to improve the effectiveness of your decision-making process to create the future you desire?

How often do you pray *before* making decisions? About proper timing?

What percentage of your decisions are based on long-term results versus short-term results?

Jesus Never Judged People By Their Outward Appearance

"My brothers, as believers in our glorious Lord Jesus Christ, don't show favoritism."

JAMES 2:1 NIV

Nobody is ever as they first appear.

Packaging is deceptive. Cereal boxes make drab cereal look like the most exciting food in the world. Billions of dollars are spent on packaging.

Don't get me wrong. Clothing is very important. Appearance sells or discourages. Proverbs 7 talks about the clothing of a prostitute. Proverbs 31 describes the clothes of a virtuous woman. Most assuredly, *it is wise to create a climate of acceptance.* Naomi, the mentor of Ruth, instructed her to put on perfume and change her clothes before she went to meet Boaz, her future husband.

But something is more important than the packaging — *the person.*

Jesus saw a scarred and weary woman who had been married five times. He saw beyond her failures and reputation. He saw her *heart.* He saw a *desire to be changed.* She was the golden bridge for Jesus to walk into the hearts of many of those people of her city. "And many of the Samaritans of that city believed on him for the saying of the woman, which testified, He told me all that ever I did" (John 4:39).

WISDOM KEY

Nothing Is Ever As It First Appears.

People saw Zaccheus as a conniving, deceptive tax collector. Jesus saw a confused man who longed for a change of heart. The people of Israel saw in Absalom a handsome, articulate leader. He was a traitor and a liar. Samson thought Delilah was the most beautiful woman he had ever met. She was the trap that destroyed his championship status.

An interesting story was shared recently by a friend of mine in Florida. She owns a clothing store. She said, "I have had ladies come to my store who looked like they did not have a penny to their name, yet they purchased thousands of dollars worth of clothing, got into their chauffeured limousine, and drove off. You could not tell what they possessed by what they wore."

Nothing is ever as it first appears.

Start listening for attitudes in people. Start listening for hurts. Don't misjudge them.

Jesus knew this.

Prayer

Father, I ask for the maturity to not judge others by their appearance but to focus on their heart and how I can affect them. Lord, You have given us the compassion to reach others. Help me to help them. In Jesus' name, amen.

Questions

In what ways do you draw out the hidden qualities in people around you?

How do you celebrate their uniqueness?

Jesus Recognized The Law Of Repetition

"*...And he took *again* the twelve, and began to tell them what things should happen unto him.*"

MARK 10:32

What you hear repeatedly, you eventually will believe.

Teachers know that the basic law of learning is *repetition*. Someone has said you must hear something sixteen times before you really believe it.

Notice the television commercials. You have seen the same ones repeatedly. Billboards advertise well-known soft drinks over and over again. Why? You must *continue hearing* and *seeing* something before you respond to it.

It simply takes *time* to absorb a message.

Jesus taught people same truths again and again. "Then spake Jesus AGAIN unto them..." (John 8:12).

Someone taught you everything you know today. You are the result of a *process*. There was a time in your life when you could not spell the word "cat" or recite numbers, but somebody was patient with you.

Great achievers understand the necessity of teaching those around them — *again and again*.

Don't expect those who are networked with you to understand everything instantly. You did not. They will not either. It takes time to grow greatness.

Jesus knew this.

Prayer

Lord, I know that what I continually hear is what I will eventually believe. Please teach me how to put this principle to use for Your glory and my success, as I teach the knowledge You have given me to

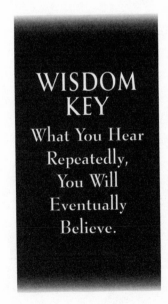

WISDOM KEY

What You Hear Repeatedly, You Will Eventually Believe.

others. Give me the grace to be patient, as they learn. In Jesus' name, amen.

Questions

What techniques do you use to reinforce what you are teaching, so others are able to learn it and apply it effectively?

How often do you repeat key points in informal conversations to help others internalize what they need to know?

Jesus Was A Tomorrow Thinker

"Remember ye not the former things,
neither consider the things of old."

ISAIAH 43:18

Become a "tomorrow thinker."

One of the great companies in Japan has a detailed plan for the next 100 years. They are *"tomorrow thinkers."*

Jesus was a "tomorrow thinker." When He met the Samaritan woman at the well, He barely mentioned that she had been married five times. *He pointed her to her future.* He said that He would give her water, and she would never thirst again.

Another remarkable illustration of "tomorrow thinking" concerns the woman caught in the act of adultery. He never discussed her sin. He simply said unto her, "Neither do I condemn thee: go, and sin no more" (John 8:11).

"Remember ye not the former things, neither consider the things of old. Behold, I will do a new thing; now it shall spring forth; shall ye not know it? I will even make a way in the wilderness, and rivers in the desert" (Isaiah 43:18,19).

Satan discusses your past. That appears to be the only information he has. Jesus discusses your *future*. He enters your life to end your past and give birth to tomorrow.

Stop taking journeys into yesterday.

Jesus concentrated on the future.

WISDOM KEY

Those Who Created Yesterday's Pain Do Not Control Tomorrow's Potential.

Prayer

Father, I thank You that You have given me a new beginning. Thank You for pointing me to my future success. You have wiped my heart clean. I will now move forward and not dwell on what was, but what is to come. In Jesus' name, amen.

Questions

Where do you want to be in your career one year from now?

What are three specific steps you need to take to get there?

What obstacles do you foresee? How will you overcome them?

Jesus Knew That Money Alone Could Not Bring Contentment

"Charge them that are rich in this world, that they be not highminded, nor trust in uncertain riches, but in the living God, who giveth us richly all things to enjoy.

1 TIMOTHY 6:17

Rich people are not always happy people.

Your hands can be full of money. Your head can be full of information, but if your heart is empty, your life is very empty.

Money is for movement, not accumulation. That is why the Bible talks about "the deceitfulness of riches."

Jesus saw this. He talked to the rich. He looked into their eyes and saw a longing for *something that money could not buy*. They came to Him late at night, when the crowds were gone.

They were lonely. "...for a man's life consisteth not in the abundance of the things which he possesseth" (Luke 12:15).

Solomon was a wealthy king. Yet he confessed, "Therefore I hated life..." (Ecclesiastes 2:17).

Think for a moment. You probably possess more today than at any time in your whole life. Do you feel more joy than you've ever had in your life? Do you laugh more now than you've ever laughed? Do you enjoy your friendships more than you ever have? Be honest with yourself.

Jesus knew "the eyes of man are never satisfied" (Proverbs 27:20). *Some things matter more than money.*

Jesus knew this.

Prayer

Father, as I achieve success, please remind me and give me the wisdom to know that money is not an "ends", but a "means". It cannot bring me happiness but giving it to

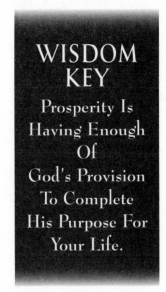

WISDOM KEY

Prosperity Is Having Enough Of God's Provision To Complete His Purpose For Your Life.

help others can. Thank You that many things matter more than money. In Jesus' name, amen.

Questions

As your income grows, how will you protect yourself from focusing on the money and what it can buy, instead of what God would have you do with it?

What kind of example do you set for your family and others around you regarding tithing and giving to the work of God's kingdom?

Jesus Knew The Power Of Words And The Power Of Silence

"He that hath knowledge spareth his words: and a man of understanding is of an excellent spirit. Even a fool, when he holdeth his peace, is counted wise: and he that shutteth his lips is esteemed a man of understanding."

PROVERBS 17:27,28

Words are not cheap.

Wars begin because of *words*. Peace comes when great men get together and negotiate and dialogue. *Words link people*. Words are the bridge into your future.

Words *created the world*. (Genesis 1:3-31.)

Words *create your world*. (Proverbs 18:21.)

Jesus said that your words reveal what kind of heart you possess. "...for of the abundance of the heart his mouth speaketh" (Luke 6:45).

Jesus said words can move mountains. (Mark 11:23.)

There is a time to *talk*. There is a time to *listen*. There is a time for *movement*. There is a time for *staying still*. When people were hungry for knowledge, Jesus spoke and taught for hours, but when He got to Pontius Pilate's hall, where truth was ignored, He was silent.

WISDOM
KEY
Silence Cannot
Be Misquoted.

Your *words* matter. Conversation matters. "But I say unto you, That every idle word that men shall speak, they shall give account thereof in the day of judgment. For by thy words thou shalt be justified, and by thy words thou shalt be condemned" (Matthew 12:36,37). Be silent about injustices to you. Be silent in discussing the weaknesses of others. Be silent in advertising your own mistakes.

Jesus knew when to talk and when to listen.

122

Prayer

Father, give me the understanding that my words are like money. Each one is to be accounted for and not spent unwisely. Teach me how to guard my tongue, and open my ears to listen. In Jesus' name, I thank You that I will know when to speak and when to listen. Amen.

Questions

In what ways do you feel you need to control your tongue and also to be a better listener?

What action will you take over the next 21 days to change how you use your tongue and how you listen?

Jesus Knew When You *Want* Something You Have Never Had, You Have To *Do* Something You Have Never Done

---

"Now the Lord had said unto Abram, Get thee out of thy country, and from thy kindred, and from thy father's house, unto a land that I will shew thee: And I will make of thee a great nation, and I will bless thee, and make thy name great; and thou shalt be a blessing."

GENESIS 12:1,2

Everything is difficult at first.

When you were beginning to crawl, it was very difficult. When you took your first step and fell, that was difficult.

Thousands will fail in life because they are unwilling to make changes. They refuse to change jobs, towns, or friendships. They stay in comfort zones. Yet thousands of others move up the ladder of happiness, because they are willing to go through a little discomfort to experience a new level in life.

Peter wanted to walk on water. Jesus saw his excitement. Then He gave a simple instruction for Peter to do something he had never done before. "And he said, 'Come.' And when Peter was come down out of the ship, he walked on the water, to go to Jesus" (Matthew 14:29).

Jesus always gave people something to do. And, it was always something *they had never done before.* He knew that their obedience was the only proof of their faith in Him.

> **WISDOM KEY**
> When You *Want* Something You Have Never Had, You Have Got To *Do* Something You Have Never Done.

Listen to the instructions to the Israelites: March around the walls of Jericho seven days in a row, and then seven times on Sunday. (Joshua 6.)

Listen to the prophet's instructions to a leper: Go dip in the Jordan River seven times. You will be healed on the seventh time. (2 Kings 5.)

Ruth left her home country of Moab to be with Naomi and she met Boaz, who changed her life forever. (Book of Ruth.)

> *Thousands will fail in life because they are unwilling to make changes.*

Elijah stretched the faith of the widow, who was down to her last meal. Two pancakes before death, he motivated her to do something she had never done: *Give* out of the little she had to someone she did not even know and *believe* the word of God's prophet for her future provision in the midst of famine. She saw the miracle come to pass. (1 Kings 17.)

Jesus knew how to stretch people's faith. He motivated them. *He helped them do things they had never done before, in order to create things they had never had.*

Jesus did new things.

Prayer

Father, help me to move out of my comfort zone and realize that in order to achieve something I have never had, I must do something I have never done before. In Jesus' name, amen.

Questions

How do you feel when you are asked to do something you have never done before?

What resources do you draw upon to be successful when you have to step out of your comfort zone?

What assistance do you provide to others when you ask them to do something they have never done before?

Jesus Permitted Others To Correct Their Mistakes

"I will forgive their iniquity, and I will remember their sin no more."

JEREMIAH 31:34

Everybody makes mistakes. Everybody.

Examine the biographies of multimillionaires. Many have experienced bankruptcy several times. They simply discovered that failure is not fatal. *Failure is merely an opinion.*

Jesus never disconnected from those who made mistakes with their lives.

Peter was one of His favorite disciples. Peter denied Him. Then he confessed his sin, and Jesus forgave him. He became one of the greatest apostles in the history of the church.

David committed adultery with Bathsheba. God forgave him. Look at Samson. He fell into sexual temptation with

Delilah, yet he is one of the champions of faith mentioned in Hebrews 11:32.

Learn to forgive *yourself.* Learn to forgive *others.* Everybody hurts somewhere. Their mistakes stay on their mind. *Give them another chance.*

Mistakes are correctable.

Jesus knew this.

Prayer

Father, just as You have forgiven me, place inside me the responsibility to forgive myself and others. You anticipated my mistakes. Teach me to give people another chance. In Jesus' name, amen.

Questions

What is one failure you have experienced in your career?

How did this failure benefit you in the end?

How do you respond when someone fails at something important to you?

WISDOM KEY
All Men Fall.
The Great Ones
Get Back Up.

Jesus Knew His Worth

---

*"A man's gift maketh room for him, and
bringeth him before great men."*

PROVERBS 18:16

Know your gift.

Many around you may never discover you. It is not really
important that they do. *What is important is that you discover
yourself, your gifts, and your talents.*

Popularity is when *other people* like you. Happiness is *when
you like yourself.*

There was an interesting scenario when Jesus visited the
home of Lazarus and his two sisters, Mary and Martha.
Martha, busy with housework, was agitated with Mary, who
was simply sitting at the feet of Jesus listening to every word
He said. When Martha complained, Jesus replied, "Mary hath
chosen that good part" (Luke 10:42).

He knew His personal worth. He knew that His own words were life. He was incredibly self-confident and *expected to be treated well.*

Jesus honored those who discerned His worth.

Jesus even reacted favorably to a woman who washed His feet. "Seest thou this woman? I entered into thine house, thou gavest me no water for my feet: but she hath washed my feet with tears, and wiped them with the hairs of her head. Thou gavest me no kiss: but this woman since the time I came in hath not ceased to kiss my feet. My head with oil thou didst not anoint: but this woman hath anointed my feet with ointment" (Luke 7:44-46).

Jesus knew His worth.

Prayer

Father, You have created me. Your Word proclaims that You have created us for Your pleasure. Teach me to accept and like myself. Happiness begins with liking who I am. In Jesus' name, amen.

WISDOM KEY

Happiness Is When You Like Yourself.

Questions

What three positive words best describe who you are?

What is one thing you do very well that you can share with others?

How will you share it with someone in the next ten days?

Jesus Never Tried To Succeed Alone

> "For by wise counsel thou shalt make thy war: and in multitude of counsellors there is safety."
>
> PROVERBS 24:6

You need people.

You need God.

Everything you have came from God. Success is a collection of relationships. Without clients, a lawyer has no career. Without patients, a doctor has no one to heal. Without a composer, a singer has nothing to sing.

Your future is connected to people, so develop people skills.

Jesus constantly talked to His Heavenly Father. He talked to His disciples. He talked to everybody. At twelve, He exchanged with the scribes and priests in the temple. He talked to tax collectors, fishermen, doctors, and lawyers. He said, "I can of mine own self do nothing" (John 5:30).

You need problem-solvers in your life.

You need a good lawyer, doctor, and financial advisor. You need your family. You need a godly pastor. You need people.

Listen to the inner voice of the Holy Spirit today. Obey every instruction.

Jesus did.

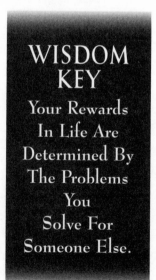

WISDOM KEY

Your Rewards In Life Are Determined By The Problems You Solve For Someone Else.

Prayer

Father, no man can do it without others. Please give me guidance and wisdom in knowing who I can turn to. I know that my life depends on other people and how I help them. In Jesus' name, amen.

Questions

What three talents do you lack that you seek in others on your team?

What do you do to allow each team member's uniqueness to shine?

Jesus Knew That Money Is Anywhere You Really Want It To Be

"The thoughts of the diligent tend only to plenteousness."

PROVERBS 21:5

Money is everywhere.

Money is anything of value. Your *time* is money. Your knowledge is money. Your *skills*, *gifts*, and *talents* are money.

Stop seeing money as merely something you carry around in your wallet. View money as *anything you possess that solves a problem for someone.*

Money is everywhere. Jesus knew that money even existed in the most unlikely places. Money is *anywhere* you really want it to be.

Colonel Sanders wanted it to be in *something he loved*, his unique fried chicken. Mohammed Ali found his financial success in boxing.

Peter was a fisherman. Tax money was needed. Jesus told him where money could be found. "Lest we should offend them, go thou to the sea, and cast an hook, and take up the fish that first cometh up; and when thou hast opened his mouth, thou shalt find a piece of money: that take, and give unto them for me and thee" (Matthew 17:27).

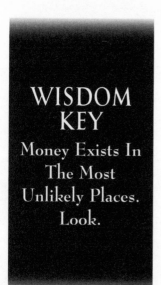

WISDOM KEY

Money Exists In The Most Unlikely Places. Look.

Do you love flowers and long to make your living owning a florist shop? That is where your money can be found.

Jesus knew that money existed *everywhere*.

Prayer

Lord, I know that You are not limited by the economic crises of this world. Please teach me how to solve problems for others and create a flow of finances necessary for my life. In Jesus' name, amen.

Questions

How wealthy are you if you consider money as anything you possess that solves a problem for someone else?

What are some ways you have helped solve a problem for someone by using this new definition of money?

Jesus Set
Specific Goals

"The wisdom of the prudent is to
understand his way."

PROVERBS 14:8

Decide what you really want.

In 1952, a prominent university discovered that only
three out of one hundred graduates had written down a clear
list of goals. Ten years later, their follow-up study showed
that 3 percent of the graduating class had accomplished
more financially than the remaining 97 percent of the class.

Those 3 percent were the *same graduates* who had *written
down their goals.* "Write the vision, and make it plain upon
tables, that he may run that readeth it" (Habakkuk 2:2).

When you decide exactly *"what"* you want, the *"how* to do
it" will emerge.

Jesus knew His purpose and mission. "For the Son of man is come to seek and to save that which was lost" (Luke 19:10).

He knew the product He had to offer. "The thief cometh not, but for to steal, and to kill, and to destroy: I am come that they might have *life*, and that they might have it more abundantly" (John 10:10).

Jesus had a sense of destiny. He knew where He wanted to go. He knew where people needed Him. (John 4:3).

Jesus knew that achievers were detail oriented. "For which of you, intending to build a tower, sitteth not down first, and counteth the cost, whether he have sufficient to finish it?" (Luke 14:28).

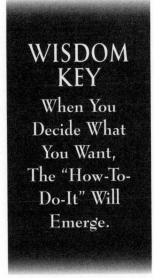

WISDOM KEY
When You Decide What You Want, The "How-To-Do-It" Will Emerge.

Take four sheets of paper. At the top of sheet number one, write, "My lifetime dreams and goals."

Write in total detail everything you would like to become, do, or have during your lifetime. *Dream your dreams in detail on paper.*

Take sheet number two and write, "My twelve-month goals."

List everything you want to get done within the next twelve months.

Take the third sheet of paper and write, "My thirty-day goals."

Write out in detail what you would like to accomplish for the next thirty days.

Take the fourth sheet of paper and write, "My ideal daily routine."

Write down the six most important things you will do in the next twenty-four hours.

The secret of your future is hidden in your daily routine. Set your goals.

Jesus knew this.

Prayer

Father, You have placed within me the ability and desire to succeed. I will plan to succeed and will write down my plan for success. I ask for insight into Your plan for my life. In Jesus' name, amen.

Questions

As you followed the above instructions for creating your dream list, how did it make you feel to see your dreams written down on paper?

What will it take to make goal setting a routine in your life?

What will you do in the next seven days to establish this routine?

Jesus Knew That Every Great Achievement Required A Willingness To Begin Small

---

"As for me, behold, my covenant is with thee, and thou shalt be a father of many nations. Neither shall thy name any more be called Abram, but thy name shall be Abraham; for a father of many nations have I made thee. And I will make thee exceeding fruitful, and I will make nations of thee, and kings shall come out of thee. And I will establish my covenant between me and thee and thy seed after thee in their generations for an everlasting covenant, to be a God unto thee, and to thy seed after thee."

GENESIS 17:4-7

Everything big starts little.

Think for just a moment. An oak tree began as an acorn. A six-foot man began as a tiny embryo in a mother's womb.

Be willing to begin small. *Start with whatever you have.* Everything you possess is a starting point. Do not be like the man in the Bible who had one talent and refused to use it. *Use whatever you have been given, and more will come to you.*

Jesus began in a stable. But He did not stay there. He went thirty years without performing miracles. But, one day He launched His first miracle. The rest is history.

David had a slingshot, but he *became* a king.

Joseph was sold as a slave, but he *became* the Prime Minister of Egypt.

The widow of Zarephath had a small pancake, but she sowed it into the work of God and created a continuous supply during the famine.

Whatever you have been given is enough to create anything you have been promised.

"For who hath despised the day of small things?" (Zechariah 4:10). "For precept must be upon precept, precept upon precept; line upon line, line upon line; here a little, and there a little" (Isaiah 28:10).

Whatever you possess today is enough to create anything else you will ever want in your future.

Jesus existed before the foundation of the world. He remembered when the earth and the human race did not even exist. That is why He did not mind the beginning in a stable.

Jesus knew *great things started small.*

Prayer

Father, I thank You that You have equipped me now with what I need to achieve success. I know that if I am willing to start small and serve others, You will honor me and elevate me to a higher position. In Jesus' name, amen.

WISDOM KEY

Whatever You Have In Your Hand Can Create Anything You Want In Your Future

Questions

Have you seen God take a small beginning and turn it into a big success in your career or for someone you know?

How have you dealt with the waiting when your career has not progressed forward as quickly as you wanted it to move?

Jesus Hurt When Others Hurt

"Rejoice with them that do rejoice, and
weep with them that weep."

ROMANS 12:15

Someone close to you is in trouble.

Have you really noticed it? Does it matter to you at all?
Everybody hurts somewhere. *When others hurt, try to feel it.*

You are a solution to somebody with a problem. Find
them. Listen for their cry.

You are their walking life jacket. You hold the key to their
lock. Feel it.

Jesus did. Jesus did not hide in the palace. He was not a
recluse. He walked where people walked. *He hurt when
people hurt.*

"And Jesus went forth, and saw a great multitude, and was moved with compassion toward them, and he healed their sick" (Matthew 14:14).

Jesus feels what you feel. "For we have not an high priest which cannot be touched with the feeling of our infirmities; but was in all points tempted like as we are, yet without sin" (Hebrews 4:15).

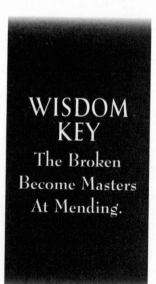

WISDOM KEY
The Broken Become Masters At Mending.

You will begin to succeed with your life when the hurt and problems of others begin to matter to you.

Several years ago, I was invited to attend a Christmas party for a large law firm here in Dallas. One of the young lawyers told an unforgettable story that night. He was the protégé of one of the great lawyers in the Midwest. This renowned lawyer won practically every case. In fact, every one of his settlements were million dollar settlements. The young lawyer simply could not figure it out. He said, "The research was normal. The reading material seemed normal.

The stack of information we had collected seemed average before he got in front of the jury."

Then he said, "This old lawyer would walk back and forth before the jury. As he talked, a transformation took place on the faces of the jury. When they came back, they always gave his client huge settlements."

That night at the Christmas party, the young lawyer told us how he probed his mentor. He said to him, "You must tell me your secret. We watch you carefully. We've read your material, but none of us in the firm can figure out why your juries return million dollar verdicts. It is a mystery we cannot unravel."

The old lawyer said, "I would like to tell you, but you really would not believe me if I did."

The young lawyer probed him month after month. For a long time the older lawyer insisted, "It really would not mean anything to you."

Finally one day when the young protégé was going to leave his firm to go to another city, the old mentor said, "Take a drive with me." They went to a grocery store. The old lawyer filled the back of his car with groceries, and they began to drive out into the country. It had snowed. It was freezing, and the icy weather was cutting. They finally drove up to a very modest, inexpensive farm house. The old mentor instructed the young lawyer to help him carry in the groceries.

When they went inside the home, the young lawyer saw a little boy sitting on a sofa. He looked closer and noticed that the little boy had both of his legs cut off. It had happened in a car accident. The old lawyer spoke to the family for a few moments and said, "Just thought I would bring a few groceries for you, since I know how difficult it is for you to get out in this kind of weather."

As they were driving back to the city, the old lawyer looked at the young lawyer and said, "It is quite simple. My clients *really do matter to me*. I *believe* in their cases. I *believe* they deserve the highest settlements that can be given. When I stand before a jury, somehow *they feel that*. They come back with the verdicts I desire. *I feel what my clients feel*. The jury *feels* what I *feel*."

> ## WISDOM KEY
> Those Who Unlock Your Compassion Are Those To Whom You Have Been Assigned.

Jesus hurt when others hurt.

Prayer

Father, please open my eyes to those around me who are hurting. Teach me that achievement and success include caring for those around me. Help me have compassion on the broken and wounded. In Jesus' name, amen.

Questions

What leaders have you observed who show compassion?

How do you incorporate compassion into your leadership style?

Jesus Was Not Afraid To Show His Feelings

"The righteous are bold as a lion."

PROVERBS 28:1

Emotions dictate world events.

An angered world leader attacks another country. Angry airline employees have a picket line at airports. A mother whose child is killed by a drunk driver launches a national campaign. Thousands are rallying to stop the abortions of millions of babies.

Feelings do matter in life.

In business, feelings are contagious. When a salesperson is excited about a product, the customer feels it and is influenced by it.

Jesus was not afraid to express Himself.

When He was infuriated, others knew it. "And the Jews' Passover was at hand, and Jesus went up to Jerusalem, and found in the temple those that sold oxen and sheep and doves...And when he had made a scourge of small cords, he drove them all out of the temple...and poured out the changers' money, and overthrew the tables" (John 2:13-15).

Jesus was deeply moved with compassion when He saw multitudes wandering aimlessly without direction. "But when he saw the multitudes, he was moved with compassion on them, because they fainted, and were scattered abroad, as sheep having no shepherd" (Matthew 9:36).

The Bible even records that Jesus wept openly. "And when he was come near, he beheld the city, and wept over it" (Luke 19:41).

I am not speaking about an uncontrollable temper, neither am I referring to someone who sobs and breaks down every time a problem occurs in their life.

Rather, I'm asking that you notice Jesus did not bottle up His emotions. He was not a robot. He

> **WISDOM KEY**
> The Problem That Infuriates You The Most Is The Problem God Has Assigned You To Solve.

was enthusiastic when He saw a demonstration of faith: He wept when He saw unbelief.

Peter, His disciple, was affected by it. The apostle Paul was set on fire by it. They changed the course of history.

Be bold in expressing your opinions. Feel strongly about the things that matter in life. You can be a marvelous influence for good.

You will always be drawn to people who are expressive. Thousands scream at rock concerts, football games, and world championship boxing matches.

Don't be a spectator of life. *Get in the arena.*

Jesus did.

Prayer

Lord, I know that passion and enthusiasm for life are keys to success. Help me to find and direct godly passion and enthusiasm into my life. Teach me to be bold in expressing my opinions and feelings. Train me to be a player in life, not a spectator. In Jesus' name, amen.

Leadership Secret 39

Questions

When was the last time you wished, after the fact, you had expressed your feelings differently in a situation?

How will you express yourself the next time you encounter a similar situation?

What can you do to learn how to incorporate expressive voice inflection, gestures, and body language into your communication style?

Jesus Knew The Power Of Habit

———

"Then said Jesus to those Jews which believed on him, 'If ye continue in my word, then are ye my disciples indeed.'"

JOHN 8:31

Great men simply have great habits.

A well-known billionaire said, "I arrive at my office at 7:00 a.m. It is a habit." Recently a best-selling novelist who has sold over one million books said, "I get up at the same time every morning. I start writing at 8:00 a.m. and I quit at 4:00 each afternoon. I do it every day. It is a habit."

Habit is a gift from God. *It simply means anything you do twice becomes easier.* It is the Creator's key in helping you succeed.

Jesus stayed busy. He traveled. He prayed for the sick. He taught and ministered. He supervised His disciples. He spoke to large crowds.

However, He had an important custom and habit. "And he came to Nazareth, where he had been brought up: AND, AS

HIS CUSTOM WAS, he went into the synagogue on the sabbath day, and stood up for to read" (Luke 4:16).

Daniel prayed three times a day. (Daniel 6:10.) The psalmist prayed seven times daily. (Psalm 119:164.) The disciples of Jesus met on the first day of each week. (Acts 20:7.)

Jesus knew *great men simply have great habits*.

Prayer

Father, teach me to develop good habits, habits that lead to success. Give me the perseverance to persist in forming habits that You desire for me. In Jesus' name, amen.

Questions

What positive habits are important to the effectiveness of your day?

What is one positive habit you would like to add to and one bad habit you would like to delete from your daily routine?

How do you plan to do this in the next 21 days?

WISDOM KEY

You Will Never Change Your Life Until You Change Something You Do Daily.

Jesus Finished What He Started

"The desire accomplished is sweet to the soul."

PROVERBS 13:19

Champions are finishers.

It is fun to be creative. It is exciting to always be giving birth to new ideas, thinking of new places to go, or launching a new product — but real champions complete things. They are *follow-through* people.

Jesus was thirty years old when He started His ministry. His ministry went for three and one-half years. He did many miracles. He touched many lives. He electrified the world through twelve men.

But, hidden in the thousands of scriptures is a golden principle that revealed Jesus' power. It happened on the horrible day of His crucifixion. He was taunted by thousands. Spears pierced His side. Spikes were driven into His hands.

Eight inches of thorns were crushed into His brow. Blood had dried on His hair. Some say four hundred soldiers left spittle running down His body.

That is when He uttered perhaps the greatest sentence ever uttered on earth: "It is finished" (John 19:30). The sins of man could be forgiven. He paid the price. The plan was complete. He was the Lamb led to the slaughter.

He was the chief cornerstone. (Ephesians 2:20.) *The Prince of Peace had come.* (Isaiah 9:6.) Our great high priest, the Son of God, was our golden link to the God of heaven. (Hebrews 4:14.)

WISDOM KEY

Your Exit Will Be Remembered Longer Than Your Entry.

Jesus was a finisher. He finished what He started. The bridge that linked man to God was complete. Man could approach God without fear.

The apostle Paul was a finisher. (2 Timothy 4:7.)

Solomon, the wisest man that ever lived, was a finisher. (1 Kings 6:14.)

One famous multi-millionaire said, "I will pay a great salary to anyone who can complete an instruction that I give to him."

Start completing *little things*. Write that "thank-you" note to your friend. Make those two telephone calls.

Get the spirit of a finisher. "He that endureth to the end shall be saved" (Matthew 10:22).

Jesus was a *finisher.*

Prayer

Father, give me the spirit of a finisher. Place the will and desire to complete what I have started. Give me Your strength to continue. In Jesus' name, amen.

Questions

What are six qualities of a *finisher*?

How many of these qualities do you possess?

What will you do in the next 30 days to be a more consistent finisher?

Jesus Was Knowledgeable Of Scripture

"Thy word is a lamp unto my feet, and a light unto my path."

PSALM 119:105

When God talks, the wise listen.

The greatest book on earth is the Bible. It has outsold every book. It is the Word of God.

It takes approximately 56 hours to read the Bible through completely. If you read 40 chapters a day, you will complete the Bible within 30 days. If you read nine chapters a day in the New Testament, you will finish reading the New Testament within 30 days. You should read the Bible systematically. Regularly. Expectantly.

Read Luke 4. When Satan presented his temptation to Jesus, He merely quoted scriptures back to him as answers.

The Word of God is powerful. "Thy word have I hid in mine heart, that I might not sin against thee" (Psalm 119:11).

The book of Proverbs has 31 chapters. Why not sit down today and start a magnificent new habit — reading this wisdom book completely through each month? Simply read chapter one on the first day of each month, chapter two on the second, and so forth.

WISDOM KEY

Faith Comes When You Hear God Talk.

The Word of God will build your faith. "So then faith cometh by hearing, and hearing by the word of God" (Romans 10:17). Faith comes when you *hear* God talk. Faith comes when you *speak* the Word of God.

The Word of God keeps you pure. "Wherewithal shall a young man cleanse his way? by taking heed thereto according to thy word" (Psalm 119:9).

Jesus knew the Word.

Prayer

Father, I know that the Bible is Your Word, and it has been given to me. I thank You, Father, for putting in my hands the means by which I can increase my faith and keep my purity. Today, I commit to read the Word and study it as the most important book in my life. In Jesus' name, amen.

Questions

How has your knowledge of God's Word impacted your effectiveness as a leader?

What will you do in the next 30 days to increase your knowledge of His Word?

Jesus Never Hurried

"In your patience possess ye your souls."
LUKE 21:19

Impatience is costly.

This is an impatient generation. Fast foods, microwave ovens, and crowded freeways reflect this philosophy.

Your greatest mistakes will happen because of impatience.

Most businesses that fail, do so because of lack of preparation and time. Great businesses do not happen overnight. Even this great country took years to become an independent nation.

Take time to grow into your business. Be deliberate with your projects. Become a "long-termer."

Life is a marathon, not a fifty-yard dash.

Champions pace themselves. They see the big picture.

Jesus refused to be rushed by the emergencies of others. There are no scriptures recorded that show where He was hurried or ever in a state of emergency.

Consider the time when word was sent to Jesus that one of His close friends, Lazarus, was sick. Mary and Martha, the sisters of Lazarus, wanted Jesus TO HURRY and pray for his healing before he died. *Jesus kept His own agenda*, an unhurried and unrushed agenda. Lazarus died. Here is the story:

"Now a certain man was sick, named Lazarus, of Bethany, the town of Mary and her sister Martha... whose brother Lazarus was sick. Therefore, his sisters sent unto him, saying, Lord, behold, he whom thou lovest is sick. When Jesus heard that, he said, This sickness is not unto death, but for the glory of God...

> *Your greatest mistakes will happen because of impatience.*

"Now Jesus loved Martha, and her sister, and Lazarus. When he had heard therefore that he was sick, he abode two days still in the same place where he was.

"Then said Martha unto Jesus, Lord, if thou hadst been here, my brother had not died.

"Jesus said unto her, Thy brother shall rise again.

"And when he thus had spoken, he cried with a loud voice, Lazarus, come forth.

"And he that was dead came forth, bound hand and foot with graveclothes: and his face was bound about with a napkin. Jesus saith unto them, Loose him, and let him go" (John 11:1-6,21,23,43,44).

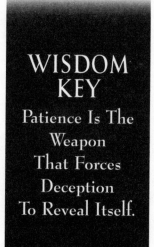

WISDOM KEY

Patience Is The Weapon That Forces Deception To Reveal Itself.

Decisiveness is powerful and magnetic, but Jesus never made decisions due to pressure tactics from others. Refuse to be intimidated by statements such as, "This is the last one available this year. If you don't buy it now, you may not get another chance."

Skilled negotiators teach that *waiting is a weapon.* Whoever is the most hurried and impatient usually ends up with the worst end of the deal.

Take time to do things right. The weakness and flaws of any plan are often buried by flurry and hurry.

Jesus knew this.

Prayer

Father, give me patience. Teach me to wait until I hear from You and know that the time is right. Thank You for giving me patience and the desire to do things correctly. In Jesus' name, amen.

Questions

As a leader, when have you experienced a situation when waiting was an effective weapon?

What types of serious errors have you seen happen as a result of impatience?

How do you guard yourself against impatience?

Jesus Went Where He Was Celebrated Instead Of Where He Was Tolerated

---

"For better it is that it be said unto thee, Come up hither; than that thou shouldest be put lower in the presence of the prince whom thine eyes have seen."

PROVERBS 25:7

Never stay where you are not valued.

Never stay where you have not been assigned. Treasure your gift. Guard well any talent God has given to you. Know this — God has prepared those to receive you when you are at the place of your assignment.

Leadership Secret 44

Jesus was unable to do any miracles in certain cities. The people doubted. Unbelief was like a cancer in the atmosphere. It stopped Him from releasing the healing flow.

He taught His disciples to disconnect from any place that did not see their worth. "And whosoever shall not receive you, nor hear your words, when ye depart out of that house or city, shake off the dust of your feet" (Matthew 10:14. See also Proverbs 25:17.)

It is foolish to waste your entire life on those who do not celebrate you. *Move on.*

Jesus did.

Prayer

Lord, I ask that You give me the wisdom and discernment to stay where I am valued and leave the places that I am not valued. Teach me not to waste my life on foolish things. In Jesus' name, amen.

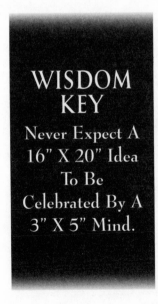

WISDOM KEY

Never Expect A 16" X 20" Idea To Be Celebrated By A 3" X 5" Mind.

Questions

What are the signs to watch for when your assignment in a place is coming to an end?

How have you responded when it became obvious your gifts and talents were not valued?

How can you prepare yourself to be ready to move when your assignment is finished?

Jesus Constantly Consulted His Heavenly Father

"Where no counsel is, the people fall: but in the multitude of counsellors there is safety."

PROVERBS 11:14

Learn to reach.

A famous billionaire of our day was trained by his father. In one of his recent books, he said that he calls his father a dozen times a week. He also telephones his own office ten to twelve times a day. He said, "If I don't constantly stay in touch with my business, it's gone." Stay in touch with your supervisor, your boss, *anyone who supervises you, mentors you, or is guiding you into something you want to accomplish.* Stay in touch regularly.

Jesus was brilliant. He was a miracle worker. He *constantly consulted* His heavenly Father. "Then answered Jesus and said

unto them, 'Verily, verily, I say unto you, The Son can do nothing of himself, but what he seeth the Father do: for what things soever he doeth, these also doeth the Son likewise'" (John 5:19).

Jesus was open to His Father about His feelings. In the garden of Gethsemane, He cried, "O my Father, if it be possible, let this cup pass from me: nevertheless, not as I will, but as thou wilt" (Matthew 26:39).

WISDOM KEY

Mentors Are Bridges To Tomorrow.

Jesus was persistent in pursuing His father. "He went away again the second time, and prayed" (Matthew 26:42). Jesus felt alone. He lived in our world. He felt the feelings you feel. He is our elder brother. *And, He was not too proud to reach for His Father.*

Know the power of connection. Create contact. Know it is the first step toward increase. *Somebody is a link to your future successes.* Tomorrow hinges on your ability to pursue them. Do it.

Jesus reached.

Prayer

Father, give me the intelligence and humility to consult those who are guiding me. Put in me the desire to remain humble and seek after You every day. Father, please keep me from becoming too proud to reach. In Jesus' name, amen.

Questions

What process do you use to stay in direct contact with your superior and/or mentor, and how often do you use it?

How well do you know your superior? What do you do to nurture that relationship?

How often do you consult your Heavenly Father for guidance regarding your work?

Jesus Knew That Prayer Generates Results

"And in the morning, rising up a great
while before day, he [Jesus] went out, and
departed into a solitary place, and
there prayed."

MARK 1:35

Prayer works.

Satan dreads your prayer link to God. He will attempt to
sabotage it in any way possible. Don't let him. *Make a daily
appointment with God.* You make appointments with your
dentist. You make appointments with your lawyer. Schedule a
specific moment with God.

You will never be the same.

Jesus prayed during crisis times. Just before His crucifixion,
He prayed three different times to His Father. (Matthew
26:44.)

He taught His disciples how to pray. There are six important words to remember as you read "The Lord's Prayer." (Matthew 6:9-13.)

1) *Praise.* "Our Father which art in heaven, Hallowed be thy name" (Matthew 6:9). Here is an important place to remember that God assigned Himself numerous names. Jehovah-Jireh (Genesis 22:14), which means "the Lord Provideth." Jehovah-Rapha (Exodus 15:26) means "the Lord that heals."

2) *Priorities.* "Thy kingdom come. Thy will be done in earth, as it is in heaven" (Matthew 6:10). This is where you ask the Lord to implement His plan for each day. Ask for His will to be done in government, on your job, in your home, and in your personal life.

3) *Provision.* "Give us this day our daily bread" (Matthew 6:11). When you pray, begin to thank God that He is providing all the finances and other resources you need for your life.

4) *Pardon.* "And forgive us our debts, as we forgive our debtors" (Matthew 6:12). Jesus instructs His disciples to release forgiveness and pardon to those who have sinned against them. What you make happen for others, God will

make happen for you. Mercy is given freely to those who *give it* freely.

5) *Protection.* "And lead us not into temptation, but deliver us from evil" (Matthew 6:13). Jesus taught His disciples to pray for total protection throughout their day.

6) *Praise.* "For thine is the kingdom, and the power, and the glory, for ever. Amen" (Matthew 6:13). Jesus taught them to end this prayer time again with praise to their heavenly Father for who He is and the power He releases into their life.

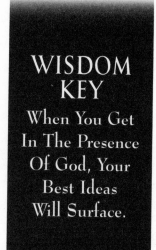

WISDOM KEY
When You Get In The Presence Of God, Your Best Ideas Will Surface.

Keep a prayer list. Set a special time each day. Have a special place, if possible.

Don't forget the *prayer of agreement.* "If two of you shall agree on earth as touching any thing that they shall ask, it shall be done for them of my Father which is in heaven" (Matthew 18:19).

Jesus *prayed.*

Prayer

Father, thank You for prayer! I know that when I am in Your presence, You will reveal Your plans and desires to me. Constantly remind me that prayer works and always will. In Jesus' name, amen.

Questions

How much time do you schedule each day to pray?

What do you do to jealously guard that time?

What special testimonies do you have about how your prayer life that has made you a better leader?

Jesus Rose Early

"Wherefore now rise up early in the morning
with thy master's servants that are come
with thee: and as soon as ye be up early in
the morning, and have light, depart."

1 SAMUEL 29:10

Champions seize their day.

Famous, successful men usually get up early. Get an early start every day. You will be amazed how much you can accomplish when others are just beginning their day.

Jesus rose early. "And in the morning rising up a great while before day, he went out, and departed into a solitary place, and there prayed" (Mark 1:35). He consulted His Heavenly Father before He consulted anyone else. He pursued the influence of God — early.

Joshua rose early. "And Joshua rose early in the morning, and the priests took up the ark of the Lord" (Joshua 6:12.)

Leadership Secret 47

Moses, the great deliverer of the Israelites, rose early. (Exodus 8:20.) Abraham, the great Patriarch of the Jewish nation, rose early. (Genesis 19:27.)

You think more clearly in the morning. You can *focus.* Your day is *uncluttered.* As you accumulate the emotions and stress of others throughout the day, the quality of your work usually deteriorates.

Your lifestyle may be an exception to this rule. Many people work all night and use their daytime for sleeping. But for the most part, most of us have discovered that the greatest hours of our day are early, uncluttered with the demands of others.

Jesus knew this.

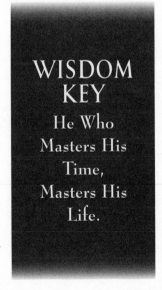

WISDOM KEY
He Who Masters His Time, Masters His Life.

Prayer

Lord, teach me to seize the day. Give me the knowledge to master my time, so that I can master my life. You have given me gifts and talents that I cannot waste in sleep. Motivate me and prompt me. In Jesus' name, amen.

Questions

What do you like to do best in the early hours of the day?

What percentage of your most productive work is accomplished before 10:00 a.m.?

What happens to your day when you don't get an early start?

Jesus Never Felt He Had To Prove Himself To Anyone

"Give not that which is holy unto the dogs, neither cast ye your pearls before swine, lest they trample them under their feet, and turn again and rend you."

MATTHEW 7:6

You are already important.

You have nothing to prove to anyone. You are the offspring of a remarkable Creator. You have the mind of Christ. Your gifts and talents have been placed within you. *Find what they are. Celebrate them.* Find ways to use those gifts to improve others and help them achieve their dreams and goals.

But never, never, never exhaust and waste your energies trying to prove something to somebody else.

Worth must be discerned.

Jesus knew this. Satan tempted Him. "If thou be the Son of God, command that these stones be made bread. But he answered and said, 'It is written, Man shall not live by bread alone, but by every word that proceedeth out of the mouth of God'" (Matthew 4:3,4).

> ## WISDOM KEY
> Those Who Do Not Discern Your Worth Are Disqualified For Relationship.

Jesus unstopped deaf ears. He opened blind eyes. He made the lame to walk. The dead were raised. Sinners were changed. Yet, the jeers of the doubters continued to scream into His ears at His crucifixion, "Thou that destroyeth the temple, and buildest it in three days, save thyself. If thou be the Son of God, come down from the cross" (Matthew 27:40).

What was Jesus' reaction? *He was confident of His worth. He knew His purpose. He refused to let the taunts of ignorant men change His plans.*

You are not responsible for anything but an honest effort to please God. *Keep focused.*

Jesus did.

Prayer

Father, I thank You for not making me responsible for anything but an honest effort to please You. Help me to remember that I do not find my value in what others think of me, but in what You think of me. In Jesus' name, amen.

Questions

How often do you find yourself feeling threatened by what others think of you as a leader?

On a score of one to ten, how would you measure your maturity level? How would your staff score you? Your associates?

Jesus Avoided Unnecessary Confrontations

"Recompense to no man evil for evil. Provide things honest in the sight of all men. If it be possible, as much as lieth in you, live peaceably with all men. Dearly beloved, avenge not yourselves, but rather give place unto wrath: for it is written, Vengeance is mine; I will repay, saith the Lord."

ROMANS 12:17-19

Stay away from unnecessary conflict.

It is exhausting. It is unproductive. Quarreling and arguing are a waste of time. Millions of dollars have been lost in negotiations because of an argumentative spirit. Warfare is costly, and nobody really wins.

Jesus knew the emptiness of anger. "And all they in the synagogue, when they heard these things, were filled with wrath, And rose up, and thrust him out of the city, and led him unto the brow of the hill whereon their city was built, that they might cast him down headlong. But he passing through the midst of them went his way" (Luke 4:28-30).

Jesus went His way.

He did not oppose them. He did not fight them. *He had other plans.* He was about His Father's business. He *focused on His own goals.* "And came down to Capernaum, a city of Galilee, and taught them on the sabbath days" (Luke 4:31).

Jesus did not withdraw into depression. He did not enter into an unnecessary dialogue with them. He didn't cower in a corner of His parent's home. *He proceeded toward His mission and purpose.*

Jesus never compromised, nor feared argument. His use of the whip in the temple reflected His strength

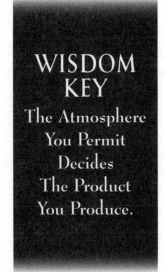

WISDOM KEY
The Atmosphere
You Permit
Decides
The Product
You Produce.

and war against evil. However, He did not waste His energy on trivial conflicts that did not merit His attention.

Learn to keep your mouth shut. "Whoso keepeth his mouth and his tongue keepeth his soul from troubles" (Proverbs 21:23).

Jesus was a peacemaker.

Prayer

Father, help me keep my mouth shut and stay in an atmosphere of peace and productivity. Do not let me wander down the path of quarreling and confusion. Keep me focused on the task at hand. In Jesus' name, amen.

Questions

How would you describe your current leadership style when dealing with anger and confrontation?

How effective are your leadership skills in avoiding or diffusing volatile situations?

Jesus Delegated

"And in those days when the number of the disciples was multiplied, there arose a murmuring of the Grecians against the Hebrews, because their widows were neglected in the daily ministration. Then the twelve called the multitude of the disciples unto them, and said, It is not reason that we should leave the word of God, and serve tables. Wherefore, brethren, look ye out among you seven men of honest report, full of the Holy Ghost and wisdom, whom we may appoint over this business. But we will give ourselves continually to prayer, and to the ministry of the word."

ACTS 6:1-4

185

Know your limitations.

It is more productive to set ten men to work than for you to do the work of ten men. *Delegation is simply giving others necessary instructions and motivation to complete a particular task.* This takes time. It takes patience. But it is a long-term benefit.

Jesus commanded the multitudes. He instructed His disciples to have the people sit down. He gave the loaves and fishes to His disciples for distribution. (Matthew 14:19.) He sent His disciples to get a donkey. (Matthew 21:2.) He gave instructions to a blind man to complete his healing. (John 9:6,7.) He sent His disciples into cities to prepare for special meals . (Mark 14:12-15.)

There are some important things you need to remember when you network with others:

1. Make a checklist of their exact responsibilities.

2. Carefully instruct them as to your exact expectations of them.

3. Give them the information and authority necessary to complete those tasks.

4. Set a specific deadline to finish the task.

5. Clearly show them how they will be rewarded for their effort.

Take the time to motivate and educate those you work with so they know exactly what you expect. *Take the time to delegate.*

Jesus did.

Prayer

Lord, place in me the wisdom and responsibility to delegate. Teach me to trust others and to know the meaning of realistic expectations. Thank You that You have given me a successful example of delegation through Your Son. In Jesus' name, amen.

Questions

On a score of one to ten how effectively do you delegate *responsibilities* to others? *Authority to others?*

What fears prevent you from delegating more effectively?

In the next 30 days what steps will you take to overcome these fears and delegate more effectively?

WISDOM
KEY
One Cannot
Multiply.

Jesus Carefully Guarded His Personal Schedule

"A wise man's heart discerneth both time and judgment."

ECCLESIASTES 8:5

Your daily agenda is your life.

You cannot save time. You cannot collect it. You cannot place it in a special bank vault. You are only permitted to *spend* it, wisely or foolishly. *You must do something with time.*

You will invest it, or you will waste it.

Many people have a hidden agenda. There will be those around you who will try to pull you "off course." There will also be those who are not seeing the "big picture." They will try to draw you into the crisis of the moment and get you off track. You must be careful to *protect your list of priorities.*

Jesus did.

As mentioned earlier, there is a fascinating story in the Bible about it. Lazarus, a close friend of Jesus, became sick. Mary and Martha, His two sisters, sent word to Jesus to come. However, "When he had heard therefore that he was sick, he abode two days still in the same place where he was" (John 11:6). Mary was upset, "Lord, if thou hadst been here, my brother had not died" (John 11:21).

Again, Jesus deliberately delayed His coming. He kept His own schedule. He tenaciously held to His agenda. He did not allow emergencies of others to get Him off track. *He guarded His list of priorities.*

Make today count. Remember the 24 golden box cars (hours) on the track of success. *If you do not control what goes into each of your 24 golden box cars, then somebody else will.*

Avoid distractions. Write your daily list of things to do. Protect your schedule. *This is your life.* Make it happen.

WISDOM KEY

Only You Know Your Priorities.

Jesus did.

Prayer

Father, give me the discretion and strength to protect my schedule. Teach me how to organize my time and give proper place to my priorities. In Jesus' name, amen.

Questions

What techniques have you found most effective to protect your daily priorities?

What will you do in the next 30 days to learn three new time management techniques?

Jesus Asked Questions To Accurately Determine The Needs And Desires Of Others

---

"Hear counsel, and receive instruction, that thou mayest be wise in thy latter end."

PROVERBS 19:20

Ask questions.

Interrogate your world. Insist on listening to the opinions and needs of others.

Almost nobody on earth listens to others or questions them.

This is a leadership secret of success.

Jesus asked questions.

Once Simon Peter went fishing. He caught nothing. When morning came, Jesus was standing on the shore. He

191

called out, "Children, have ye any meat?" (John 21:5). *He assumed nothing. He pursued information.*

Their answer was His entry point into their life. He had something they needed. *He had information.*

His question was a link to their future. *It was the bridge for their relationship.* He then instructed them, "Cast the net on the right side of the ship, and ye shall find..." (John 21:6).

WISDOM KEY

Information Is The Difference Between Your Present And Your Future.

Document the needs of others. Keep a Rolodex. Keep a notebook of their needs and desires. What are your customers' needs today? Are you *really listening* to them? Do they really feel you are listening to them? Most employees feel that their bosses really do not hear their complaints. Most employers feel that their employees do not interpret them correctly.

Jesus pursued information.

Leadership Secret 52

Prayer

Father, open my eyes and ears to see and hear information correctly. Constantly remind me of the importance of information and how it can determine my success. In Jesus' name, amen.

Questions

How frequently do you ask your staff or associates what they need or desire?

How effective are you in asking your internal and external customers the right questions to determine their *real* needs, not just what they *think* they want?

What will you do over the next 90 days to improve your questioning skills?

Jesus Always Answered Truthfully

"...Who keeps his oath even when it hurts."
PSALM 15:4 NIV

Be truthful.

Someone has said, "Tell the truth the first time, and you will never have to try and remember what you said." Truth will always outlast the storms of slander and false accusation.

Never misrepresent your product to a customer.

Carefully build and forge before your family the picture of total truth.

Nothing is more important in life than believability. When you lose that, you have lost the essence of favor, love, and success.

Jesus was Truth.

"I am the way, the truth, and the life: no man cometh unto the Father, but by me" (John 14:6). His integrity

194

intimidated hypocrites. They reacted to His purity. Honesty is a force. It will destroy mountains of prejudice and fear in a single blow. "God is not a man, that he should lie; neither the son of man, that he should repent: hath he said, and shall he not do it? or hath he spoken, and shall he not make it good?"(Numbers 23:19).

Prayer

Father, teach me to guard my mouth and let only truth come out of it. Since truth cannot be changed, truth that I speak can change the world. In Jesus' name, amen.

Questions

What situations have you encountered in your career where the truth may have hurt, but your integrity was at stake if you didn't speak the truth?

What godly advice on speaking truth would you give a new graduate just starting in the business world today?

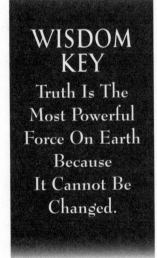

WISDOM KEY
Truth Is The Most Powerful Force On Earth Because It Cannot Be Changed.

Jesus Stayed In The Center Of His Expertise

"And also that every man should eat and drink, and enjoy the good of all his labour, it is the gift of God."

ECCLESIASTES 3:13

Do what you do best.

What do you *love* to do? What do you *love* to talk about? What would you rather *hear* about more than anything else on earth? What would you do with your life *if money was not a factor?* What do you do *best* of all?

Your joy is determined by doing what you love.

Jesus associated with fishermen. He talked to tax collectors. Doctors and lawyers and religious leaders were regularly in His life. *But He never wavered from His focus.* "How God anointed Jesus of Nazareth with the Holy Ghost and with

196

power: who went about doing good, and healing all that were oppressed of the devil; for God was with him" (Acts 10:38).

Jesus knew His mission.

He stayed focused. I really believe that *broken focus is the real reason men fail.*

Some people take jobs because they are convenient or close to their home. One man told me that he had spent his entire life working on a job that made him miserable.

"Why have you worked there for twenty-seven years then?" I asked.

"It's only ten minutes from my house," he replied. "And in three years I will receive a gold watch. I don't want to leave too early and miss my gold watch."

What you love is a clue to your calling and talent.

Jesus knew this.

WISDOM KEY
The Only Reason Men Fail Is Broken Focus.

Prayer

Father, You have placed within me a specific design and purpose. Teach me to stay focused and perform with excellence the talents You have given me. In Jesus' name, amen.

Questions

What did you discover about your own center of expertise when you answered the questions in the first paragraph?

How do you keep yourself focused?

Jesus Accepted The Responsibility For The Mistakes Of Those Under His Authority

---

"And be ye kind one to another, tenderhearted, forgiving one another, even as God for Christ's sake hath forgiven you."

EPHESIANS 4:32

People make mistakes.

This is not a perfect world. Your business is not a perfect business. Your friendships are not flawless. Those who work with you will make errors.

Remember, *you are mentoring those who receive your instructions.* They are in a process of growing. They are learning. They will stumble and make mistakes. Some of them will be costly.

I read an interesting story some years ago. An executive secretary to the president of a large corporation made a mistake, costing the company $50,000.00. She was devastated and brought her letter of resignation to the president explaining, "I realize what a dumb thing I did. I am very sorry. I know that it cost the company $50,000.00. Here is my letter of resignation."

"Are you crazy?" he thundered. "I have been teaching you and educating you every week. Now you have made a big mistake. I have just invested $50,000.00 in your education, and you're going to leave? No, ma'am. You are not going to leave. You have cost me too much to lose my investment in you." She stayed and became an extraordinary executive.

WISDOM KEY

Forgiveness Makes A Future Possible.

Peter denied the Lord, yet Jesus lovingly said, "Simon, Simon, behold, Satan hath desired to have you, that he may sift you as wheat: but I have prayed for thee, that thy faith fail not: and when thou art converted, strengthen thy brethren" (Luke 22:31,32).

Great leaders accept the responsibility for their troops. If you are going to have extraordinary success in your business, be strong and courageous enough to take the responsibility for the mistakes of those who are in the process of learning from you. Don't whine. Don't complain. Be strong.

Jesus was our supreme example.

Prayer

Father, teach me to forgive and always remind me that no man or woman is perfect. Give me the courage and foresight to accept responsibility for those for whom I am responsible. Teach me to follow in the footsteps of Jesus. In Jesus' name, amen.

Questions

When a staff member makes a serious mistake, how do you handle it? Have you ever asked a staff member to forgive you for the way you reacted to their mistake?

When a mistake is questioned by your superiors, do you defend your staff or blame them?

Do you pray for your staff on a regular basis? How has it made a difference in your relationship with them?

Jesus Pursued The Mentorship Of More Experienced Men

"Ointment and perfume rejoice the heart: so doth the sweetness of a man's friend by hearty counsel."

PROVERBS 27:9

Mentors are teachers in your life.

Your mentors are not perfect people. They simply have experienced life and are capable of transferring that knowledge to you. Your mentor can be older or younger than yourself. Your mentor is *anyone capable of growing and increasing your life*.

Show me your mentors, and I can predict your future. "A wise man will hear, and will increase learning; and a man of understanding shall attain unto wise counsels" (Proverbs 1:5).

Jesus sought knowledge. When He was twelve, He pursued the teachers of His day. "And it came to pass, that after three days they found him in the temple, sitting in the midst of the doctors, both hearing them, and asking them questions" (Luke 2:46).

Ruth listened to the advice of Naomi. Esther listened to Mordecai. David sat at the feet of Samuel. Joshua received instructions from Moses. Timothy was mentored by Paul. Elisha ran to stay in the presence of Elijah.

"And when they saw him, they were amazed: and his mother said unto him, Son, why hast thou thus dealt with us? behold, thy father and I have sought thee sorrowing. And He said unto them, How is it ye sought me? wist ye not that I must be about my Father's business?" (Luke 2:48,49).

WISDOM KEY
Know Greatness When You Get In The Presence Of It.

Solomon said, "Where no counsel is, the people fall: but in the multitude of counsellors there is safety" (Proverbs 11:14). "He that walketh with wise men shall be wise: but a companion of fools shall be destroyed" (Proverbs 13:20).

Listen to your mentors. Sit in their presence. Purchase their tapes. Absorb their books. *One sentence can be the golden door to the next season of your life.*

Jesus was teachable.

Prayer

Father, give me the humility and willingness to listen to the experienced and the wise. Thank You for giving me the discernment to know when I should open my ears and when I should not. You have given me the opportunity to learn and achieve. In Jesus' name, amen.

WISDOM KEY

The First Step Toward Success Is The Willingness To Listen.

Questions

What three people have had the greatest impact on your career?

List one key nugget of wisdom you have learned from each one.

How often do you communicate with your current mentor?

Jesus Did Not Permit Those He Led To Show Disrespect

"For where envying and strife is, there is confusion and every evil work."

JAMES 3:16

Never tolerate strife.

Strife will not go away voluntarily. You must confront it. *You will never correct what you are unwilling to confront.* Always name rebellion for what it is. Pinpoint rebellion. When there is a rebel in your company, discern it. *Mark those who create strife.* "Now I beseech you, brethren, mark them which cause divisions and offences contrary to the doctrine which ye have learned; and avoid them" (Romans 16:17).

Jesus loved people. He cherished hours with His disciples. He was a listener. He was gracious and humble. But, He was quite aware of something that every successful person should remember: *familiarity can often incubate disrespect.*

One day Peter began to feel extra comfortable with Jesus. Comfortable enough to correct Him. "Then Peter took him, and began to rebuke him, saying, Be it far from thee, Lord: this shall not be unto thee" (Matthew 16:22).

Suddenly, the gentle and kind Jesus revealed His nature of steel. He was immovable. He was unshakable. In a single stroke of communication, He stripped Peter of his cockiness. Peter had *presumed* on the relationship. Jesus had *never* given him the authority to correct Him. "But he turned, and said unto Peter, Get thee behind me, Satan: thou art an offence unto me: for thou savourest not the things that be of God, but those that be of men" (Matthew 16:23).

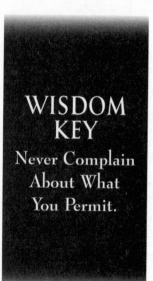

WISDOM KEY

Never Complain About What You Permit.

Jesus did not tolerate disrespect.

You see, rebellion is contagious. One rebel can destroy thousands of people. *Confront those who cause contention.* Do not expect them to fade into the sunset. They never do.

Your business success depends on a peaceful and happy climate. You must constantly be aware of signs of discontent. Deal with it before it spreads like a virus throughout your organization.

One of the famous staff managers for a United States President says, "I manage by the acorn management philosophy. I look for problems when they are the size of an acorn. I refuse to watch them grow into oak trees."

People rarely respect and follow anyone they are capable of intimidating, dominating, or manipulating.

Jesus knew this.

Prayer

Lord, grant me the discernment and courage to keep those under my authority from being disrespectful. Teach me how to respond to them in a manner that will defuse their wrong attitudes and guide them toward higher standards. In Jesus' name, amen.

Questions

When was the last time you had to counsel with a staff member about showing proper respect?

Did you handle it in public or private?

How did the staff member respond?

How did you use the situation to accomplish something positive?

Jesus Respected The Law Of Sowing And Reaping

"Be not deceived; God is not mocked: for whatsoever a man soweth, that shall he also reap."

GALATIANS 6:7

Everything begins with a seed to sow.

Someone plants a small acorn. It becomes the mighty oak tree. A small kernel of corn is planted. It produces two cornstalks. Each stalk produces two ears of corn. Each ear of corn contains over seven hundred kernels of corn. From that one small kernel of corn, a seed, 2,800 more kernels are created.

Look at *seed as anything that can multiply and become more.* Love is a seed. Money is a seed. Everything you possess can be planted back into the world as a *seed.*

Your seed is anything you give that benefits another person, a smile...time...a word of encouragement...money.

Your harvest is anything God gives back that benefits you, joy...peace of mind...a friend...finances.

Sowing a seed in faith simply means to give *something, having faith God will honor His Word and give you a harvest* of what you have given to Him.

Sowing a seed in faith is using what you have been given to obtain what God has promised. If you sow the seed of diligence on your job, your harvest will be promotion. "The soul of the sluggard desireth, and hath nothing: but the soul of the diligent shall be made fat" (Proverbs 13:4). "He becometh poor that dealeth with a slack hand: but the hand of the diligent maketh rich" (Proverbs 10:4).

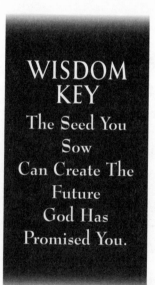

WISDOM
KEY
The Seed You
Sow
Can Create The
Future
God Has
Promised You.

When you sow love into your family, you will reap love. When you sow finances into the work of God, you will reap God's blessings and provision on your finances.

Jesus taught that giving was the beginning of blessings. "Give, and it shall be given unto you; good measure, pressed down, and shaken together, and running over, shall men give into your bosom. For with the same measure that ye mete withal it shall be measured to you again" (Luke 6:38).

This same scripture illustrates another incredible principle: *Whatever you are, you will create around you.* I am Irish. What will I create? Irishmen. What will a musician create? Musicians. What will a watermelon create? Watermelons. When you give, people around you start wanting to give to you.

It is simple, explosive, and undeniable.

Jesus taught the 100-fold principle. "And Jesus answered and said, Verily I say unto you, There is no man that hath left house, or brethren, or sisters, or father, or mother, or wife, or children, or lands, for my sake, and the gospel's, But he shall receive an hundredfold now in this time, houses, and brethren, and sisters, and mothers, and children, and lands,

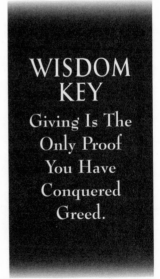

WISDOM KEY

Giving Is The Only Proof You Have Conquered Greed.

with persecutions; and in the world to come eternal life" (Mark 10:29,30).

Everything you have, came from God. *Everything you will receive* in your future will come from God. He is your total source for everything in your life. Never forget this.

He wants you to have His blessings. "For the Lord God is a sun and shield: the Lord will give grace and glory: no good thing will he withhold from them that walk uprightly" (Psalm 84:11). "Beloved, I wish above all things that thou mayest prosper and be in health, even as thy soul prospereth" (3 John 2).

WISDOM KEY

When You Let Go Of What Is In Your Hand, God Will Let Go Of What Is In His Hand For You.

The secret of your future is determined by the seeds you sow today.

When you open your heart, God will open His windows. Never forget that 10 percent of your income is holy seed. It is called *"The Tithe."* "Bring ye all the tithes into the storehouse, that there may be meat in mine house, and prove me now herewith, saith the Lord of hosts, if I will not open you the windows of heaven, and pour you out a blessing, that there shall not be room enough to receive it. And I will rebuke the devourer for your sakes, and he shall not destroy the fruits of your ground" (Malachi 3:10,11).

You can give your way out of trouble. Your seed can create what God has promised you. Remember, God has a Son, Jesus. He *sowed* Him in the earth to *produce* a family. *Millions are born again because of His best Seed.*

Jesus knew this.

Prayer

Father, thank You for showing me that if I plant good seed, I will reap a great harvest. I am expecting the miracle of harvest You promised. Lord, keep this principle of sowing and reaping always before me and teach me to honor it always. In Jesus' name, amen.

Questions

What seeds has God given you to sow into the lives of your staff and associates?

Can you describe an instance when you planted words of encouragement in a difficult staff member that resulted in a happier, more productive worker? Why not try it today?

PART II

HOW TO ENJOY
THE WINNING LIFE

HOW TO ENJOY THE WINNING LIFE

Success brings happiness, and happiness is basically feeling good about yourself, your life, and your plans. Or, as a friend of mine says, "Success is *joy!*"

Two forces are vital to happiness: your *relationships* and your *achievements.*

The Gospel also has two forces: the *Person* of Jesus Christ and the *principles* He taught. You see, one is the *Son* of God, the other is the *system* of God.

One is the *life* of God, the other is the *law* of God. One is the *King,* the other is the *kingdom.* One is an *experience with God,* the other is the *expertise of God.* One is *heart*-related, the other is *mind*-related.

Salvation is experienced *instantaneously,* but the wisdom keys are learned *progressively.*

Both forces are absolute essentials to total success and happiness.

You may be a *church member* and religious in your experience, but you will live in continuous periods of *frustration without the knowledge of the success laws established in the Scriptures.* The *expertise* of God is a must in situations that arise in our daily living.

You may be a *non*-church member or an unbeliever. You may experience tremendous social, financial, and family success and achievements through simple application of the Laws of Life as set forth in the Bible. But without an *experience* with Jesus Christ, the Son of God, you will always sense a vast void and loneliness, an awareness that "something is missing in my life."

Job promotion, financial empire building, and social acceptance will heighten and accentuate the emptiness, rather than fill it. *God has not created a world He would not be needed in.*

Success is the *progressive achievement of God-intended goals.* It is attainment of the will and plans *of the Father.* It is important that we have a *dream* or purpose in our lives. Joseph dreamed a dream. Jesus had purpose.

Our goals should be ordered of the Lord. David wanted to build the temple, but his desire was not a God-intended goal. Solomon was the builder God had chosen. Sometimes our personal desires are contradictory to God's plans.

How To Enjoy The Winning Life

How do we know the difference? *Consultation* with the Father. Through studying the *Bible* and private prayer time, we discover God's plans. Usually, they are revealed step-by-step.

If your desire for something PERSISTS, it probably is an indication that God wants you involved in that particular accomplishment. For example, God chose Solomon to build, but David PREPARED the materials.

Obviously, we must *know* what God wants us to do *before* we can do it. LOOK for signs. LISTEN to the Spirit. Evaluate. Cultivate *instant response* to the voice of God. *Eliminate the time-wasters* in your life. Concentrate on your God-connection.

WISDOM KEY
Never Speak Words That Make The Enemy Think He's Winning.

Reject all feedback and comments that breed doubt and defeat. Jesus did not give the same quality time to the Pharisees that He gave to the Samaritan woman. He discerned the *purpose of every conversation*, whether it came from a hungry heart or a critical attitude.

The WINNER knows the power of words. Refuse to release words of defeat, depression, and discouragement. Your words are life. Express hope and confidence in God. Get so excited over planning your triumphs, you don't have time to complain over past losses.

The WINNER expects opposition. Recognize that adversity has advantages. It reveals the depth of friendships. It will force you to dig for more accurate information. It will help you decide what you really believe.

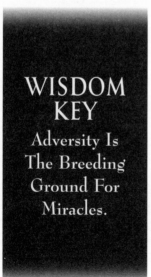

WISDOM KEY

Adversity Is The Breeding Ground For Miracles.

The WINNER expects special wisdom to come. "If any of you lack wisdom, let him ask of God, that giveth to all men liberally, and upbraideth not; and it shall be given him" (James 1:5). Wisdom is the *ability to interpret a situation through God's eyes.* Wisdom is seeing what God sees. Understanding and wisdom are the golden keys to mastering every circumstance in life. It comes through WORD STUDY. "The entrance of thy words giveth light; it giveth understanding unto the simple" (Psalm 119:130).

WINNERS are different from the "crowd." *Never* justify failure. Refuse to bog down in placing blame on others. *Reach UP for the key OUT.*

WHEN YOU MAKE UP YOUR MIND, IT'S JUST A MATTER OF TIME!

Additional copies of *Leadership Secrets of Jesus*
and the following other books by Dr. Mike Murdock
are available from your local bookstore.

The Making of a Champion
The One-Minute Pocket Bible for Men
The One-Minute Pocket Bible for Women
The One-Minute Pocket Bible for Teenagers
The One-Minute Pocket Bible for Business Professionals
Wisdom for Crisis Times
Wisdom for Winning
Secrets for Winning at Work

Tulsa, Oklahoma